To Natalie,

with all best wishes,

Nicky

MW00980884

The
Universal Language

Nicky Gluch

First edition: Sydney, 2019.
Publisher: Sydney School of Arts & Humanities
15-17 Argyle St Millers Point 2000 Australia
www.ssoa.com.au

The Universal Language
ISBN: 978-0-6483216-7-5 (print)
        978-0-6483216-8-2 (ebook)

All dates, place names and events in this memoir are factual. How-
ever, in accordance with the wishes of some participants, all names
have been changed in order to protect personal privacy.
Cover design & formatting Ferdinando Manzo
Typeset Times New Roman
Printed and bound by Lightning Source, 2019.

National Library of Australia Cataloguing-in-Publication data:
Nicky Gluch, author, 2019.
The Universal Language / Gluch, Nicky.
ISBN   978-0-6483216-7-5 (print)
          978-0-6483216-8-2 (ebook)

Dedication

In memory of Evan Higgins

Acknowledgements

The intention to write this book existed for several years before I had either the opportunity or the correct forum in which to write it. The opportunity was one I grasped in answer to *When life gives you lemons* ... so perhaps I should thank my lemon givers, but the book would probably have gone nowhere without the support and encouragement of the Sydney School of Arts and Humanities, specifically the Our Memoir Group (OMG) into which I wandered one Tuesday morning.

The director, Dr Christine Williams, made us hold hands and at first I panicked that the group wasn't for me! But the weekly writing exercises and Christine's constructive criticism kept me going back and, indeed, in these months alone in London, I've come to miss the hand holding ritual!

My hand from afar was Lawrence Goodstone, who offered to read my work to the group in my absence. It is because of him that the book continued past Chapter 4 and then it is because of Christine, who offered to publish an extract when I was 6 months in, that the rest of the book took form.

Of course this book would not exist if not for the people with whom I spent my time in Israel. As they are protected by pseudonyms within, I shall thank them accordingly: to Leanora, Tanya and Nell, and to Jim, Robert, Luc, Misha, Samer, Liat and Claire, thank you for leaving me with the most wonderful memories! Thank you for inspiring me, and giving me stories to tell. To Prof Jack, I hope this book somewhat resembles what you meant when you said 'Do something that matters' and to Sandy, thank you for your friendship these past five years. It has meant the world to me.

My heartfelt thanks to Claire Foster-Gilbert for agreeing to write the Foreword. Wishing you a *refuah shlema*.

To my sister, for her love. That easier times will be around the corner.

To my Dad, for having supported me at every step of the way. Thank you for having encouraged your daughters to have enquiring minds and (within reason) not limiting the scopes of our freedom.

And to my Mum, my correspondent. Thank you for writing to me, most importantly, and for being a sounding board, a keen ear, questioner, supporter. For teaching me to love words, and to play with language. For passing on your love of books, with all the other gifts you've given me. This book is as much yours as it is mine.

Contents

Foreword

This book is full of coincidences so I'm pleased to claim its first: my meeting with Nicky. Nicky came and conducted our modest little choir as a favour to our director, who had been called away suddenly. None of us had met her before. Indeed our director hadn't, asking her on the recommendation of a trusted friend.

I was immediately struck by Nicky's presence as she stood, exposed as only a conductor can be, encouraging our diffident selves to give what we had. Sometimes it has seemed to me that the conductor is the player, the choir and orchestra her instruments, responding to her call to: make this sound, now that, in this time, now that. But Nicky did not command with such confident machismo. She led as a wounded healer or servant leader might lead. She seemed utterly vulnerable and exposed; she somehow showed all of herself to us; it was up to us to respond, making a conscious and free choice to do so. Music was the thing; not Nicky, not us. In this strange, free and vulnerable encounter, hitherto unseen and unknown possibilities emerged. The music we might make had never been heard before, though it was written in the 16th century.

Nicky's conducting style reminded me of a study that Czech philosopher Alice Koubova drew upon when she was writing about the creative potential of enactive, performative encounter. In the study, students in turn entered an empty space with an audience made up of the other students. The one in the middle of the performing space was given nothing to do, and he was not to contact the audience visually or physically. The audience was to support him with its favourable attention. The experiment was repeated over a year, during which time the students reported moving from initial terror at their exposure, to allowing their hidden selves to be born on stage and contribute to the performance. Everyone became surprised and delighted at the unexpected creations that emerged from encounters that were pre-eminently acts of bravery and trust.

It did not surprise me, though it intrigued me, to learn in the pub after our choir rehearsal that Nicky is researching leadership in conducting. How obvious it seems, but like many things that make obvious sense when they are pointed out, it hadn't been thought of by us, not really, before Nicky started to ask the questions.

This book is full of questions that are both deeply personal: a young woman exploring her inner journey with a merciless commitment to truth; and also exploring the journey of that deep, alive, pulsating-with-emotion, impossible-to-encapsulate-or-define place, Israel-Palestine. Her lyrical writing expresses Nicky's vulnerable musicality, and it opens up hitherto unseen and unknown possibilities, in herself and in the country she travels through. I recommend you read it twice, the second time slowly.

I recognise the wisdom of Nicky's willingness to allow, not control, her own destiny and that of Israel-Palestine in my own fields of public moral philosophy and theology. I began my career as a research fellow working, at the Centre of Medical Law and Ethics, King's College, London, on the ethics of medical research on humans. The approach I developed, drawing on the work of jurisprudent Ronald Dworkin and moral philosopher Sophie Botros, was a rigorous, systematic one, allowing each research project to be interrogated from a goal-based, utilitarian perspective (was the research seeking a morally desirable goal? was it designed in such a way that it would achieve that goal?); a duty-based perspective (what would the research subjects have to undergo for the research goal to be attained? was it morally right for them so to be asked?); and a right-based perspective (was consent being sought? how?). This three-pronged approach to addressing moral questions in medical ethics had many advantages: it was rigorous, ensuring important moral issues were addressed; it recognised that there were often competing moral claims made evident when judgements had to be made between them, without dictating which should take precedent; and it helped the moral decision-maker to be clear about how she was navigating the territory. She could give an account of how and why she made the decision she did: what moral concerns she judged should take precedence, and what was the moral cost of her choice.

I use this rigorous, three-pronged approach in moral decision-making to this day. But what the approach doesn't do is address matters of the heart, and these are paramount in our human lives, affecting every decision we make. A mother sits by the bed of her dying child. She must decide whether to switch off his life support. She is not thinking about goal-based utilitarian solutions to her problem, nor is she wondering what the duty-based Kantian Categorical Imperative would dictate. Her heart is breaking. And our rigorous methods had no language of comfort or compassion that could bring her solace.

At the time I worked there, the Centre was vociferous in its refusal to allow a place for religion in medical ethics. For the academic philosophers and lawyers at the Centre, religion was an irrational, absolutist naysayer, claiming higher knowledge from a non-existent deity who issued rules and could not be gainsaid. But I was to find, as I moved from the merely intellectual rigour of King's to the Board for Social Responsibility of the Church of England as its medical and environmental ethics adviser, that here, at any rate, was a language of the heart that recognised human need, and did not expect fallible people, often in deep psychological pain, to come up with the right answers. You don't know what to do, so you pray. You cannot see a way forward, so you ask for help. You tried to do the right thing, but know that however well-meaning you were, you did not get it right; could not have got it right; so you say sorry. Things turned out well for you due to far more than your mere skill and ingenuity, so you say thank you. Far from the academics' caricature, religion was of the greatest possible service to moral philosophy. And in its recognition of our heartfelt need, its willingness not to assume control of our destinies, lay the creative possibilities of hitherto unseen and unknown responses. Genuinely new ways of perceiving – in healthcare, in ecology – emerged.

Later, I came to Westminster Abbey to create an Institute to serve and support the public servants working in the institutions of government that were the Abbey's neighbours on Parliament Square in London. Westminster Abbey sits on one side of Parliament Square, with the Houses of Parliament, the legislature, to the east; the Treasury and other government departments, the executive, to the north, and the Supreme Court, the judiciary, to the west. It was questionable whether these institutions that rule and run a country of many faiths and no faith would want help from a church; but – to my surprise, I confess – there was a strong response to the offer; a thirst for reflective depth which the public servants felt the Abbey could offer them; a desire to reconnect to the vocation for public service that was so quickly lost in the busy task of enacting it. And provided we didn't proselytise (but this is the Church of England: we are curled over backwards embarrassed to declare our faith), our facility to connect with depth was welcomed.

And it has genuinely helped. For unlike the pitiless public whom our politicians and civil servants serve, religion expects human imperfection in them; in all of us. Again, new possibilities emerge as we surrender control, acknowledging our vulnerabilities, owning our humanity.

Religion faces the very great danger of altogether removing autonomy from humans who only too often want to be infantilised, wanting mummy and daddy to tell us what to do, to make it all right. (But we make the same mistake in politics: we vilify politicians so readily because we want them to make everything all right and are constantly disappointed. A 2014 study showed that 60% of us expect more of our government than we do of God.) Religion can reduce our respect for and trust in our own rationality. If a foolish person takes upon himself the role of leader in that religion, arrogating the task of interpretation of the numinous, playing on our infantilisable selves, becoming, in effect, a god, then religion becomes a tinderbox for far worse wrong doing than puny human rationality could propose.

That is a risk. But without religion there is no reaching beyond our grasp. And faced with impossible tasks, such as reconciling the powerful moral logic of the Israelis with the heartbreaking story of the Palestinians, or realising the full potential of one brave woman's life in truthful service, we must repent, surrender, listen, follow, say thank you.

Claire Foster-Gilbert
Director, Westminster Abbey Institute
London, May 2019.

Introduction

When I began writing this book in Sydney in May, 2018, I could never have predicted finishing it in the same week of the year as I left Israel in 2014. Indeed, that is the wonderful thing about coincidence: planned, such events would seem contrived, yet when they happen, with the hand which has caused them unseen, there is no greater feeling. I remember experiencing it for the first time as a seven-year-old, when my family were living in Boston. Mum had taken my sister and me to a movie, a rare treat in those days, and as we took the bus back, about half-way to home, who got on but Dad!? I remember Mum's joy, for my parents' marriage has been blessed by such occurrences, and thus from her I learnt to delight in them.

A coincidence that occurs outside the scope of this book, yet in many ways gets to its essence, is worth repeating here. In November 2018, I went to Oslo for a meeting. Finding myself with a free evening, I decided to attend a symphony concert but, for lack of a smart-phone, was unable to book a ticket. Deciding to take a chance at buying one at the door, I turned up at the concert hall and as I approached the ticket desk, was stopped by a woman who asked, '*Vil du ha en fribillett?*' Not knowing if she was asking me if I wanted a spare ticket, or if I had one, I shook my head, to which she replied in fluent English, 'Do you want a free ticket?'

Finding that her companion hadn't been able to join her, I gratefully accepted, before realising that I would now have to sit next to this mystery woman for the whole concert. What would we talk about?

Everything, as it turned out – from our backgrounds playing Baroque instruments, to the fact we were both writers. She was interested in what had brought me to Oslo, and told me of her own PhD, before the house lights dimmed and the music silenced our conversation.

The piece before interval had been composed by Bartok, which led the woman to tell me of her Hungarian heritage. I was surprised. Her English had sufficiently fulfilled the, 'Where do you come from?' question that I hadn't thought to dig further.

'So your family went from Hungary to England?' I now asked. 'Yes,' she replied, 'and Australia and South America, and Auschwitz, as happens …'

'Oh,' I said, 'I'm sorry. I've always been grateful that my family left Europe before the war.'

And between the gaps, we understood, that out of the all the people I could have met that day, I'd crossed paths with one of the 1500 Jews in Norway (less than half of 1% of the population) brought together not by faith, or politics or even ed-ucation, but by music. 'Doesn't that prove what your book's about?' the woman asked. I couldn't but agree.

Most simply put, this book is about the six months I spent in Israel in 2013-14 and why my time there led me to pursue a career in music, rather than medicine. It is drawn from emails I sent my mum during this period, and in this way is very much a story of a nineteen-year-old student living and expe-riencing the world alone for the first time. It is not enough, however, to say that Israel is merely its setting, for it is also its subject, though this book is a product of what happened, not when I was there but after I left.

In July 2014, a war broke out between Israel and Gaza. My concern, of course, was for my friends who still lived there, while the concern of my friends in Australia was that I ever had. I was marked, supposed by them to be on the side of Is-rael, an enemy to their left-wing politics, and no longer able to be their friend. What depressed me, more than the hatred, was that no one ever stopped to ask me how I felt about Israel, the nation, or Israelis I had met. What I had seen there, done there, if I did or didn't support the military operation. I was a Jew who had lived in Jerusalem, so to them it was enough to condemn me.

Two years later, I was sitting in a dining hall of an American university. I was there for a summer workshop and bemoan-ing the fact that my then-boyfriend had still not applied for his visa to visit me in Australia. Of course this story required that I explain why he needed one. He was Israeli, I said, and on that word alone a student began to shout at me across the table.

The humour is that my boyfriend, without any political motivation, had acted antithetically to the Israeli government agenda. His allegiance was to science, alone, his Israeli passport a matter of circumstance and, I imagine, happily discarded if another had ever been offered. But I never got to say this, not that I should have had to, for the real question was why this student, like my friends back home, felt so entitled to judge me for something that they had no direct connection to.

And why, for such intelligent people, did they believe that the news was told without bias? And, for that matter, that there was nothing more to the country than what the media portrayed.

Those painful episodes are what motivated me to write this book. It is an attempt, through memoir, to show what Israel meant to me. It seeks to uncover, rather than convert, to reveal through story some issues of politics and religion, but it is, most deeply, personal. This is Israel through my eyes, as a student, an Australian, a woman, a Jew. The view is a product of when it is set, for Jerusalem has changed much since 2014, and it is equally a product of when it was written.

Though I began the book in Sydney, I finished it in London. Though I'd started writing in May, I had left for Israel in August, but by November the book had caught up with itself. I was writing about events exactly five years after they happened. In this way the book is like a mobius strip: the events as they occurred and the events as they are written inextricably linked, though the two shall never meet.

Through fragments, the book unfolds, snapshots which at the end I hope will provide a complete picture, yet one that makes you want to look more closely at the pieces. To find what lies between the gaps, for that is the realm of possibility!

As the concept of language is central to the text, I have included Hebrew words and phrases where I felt they were relevant. Most often, translations are provided as footnotes, unless the phrases are integral to the narrative, in which case the English immediately follows. That those fluent in Hebrew may find my use of it crude is deliberate, for just as a child speaks in simple sentences, so my Hebrew at the time was similarly immature. And never then did I imagine the many other languages I'd have cause to stumble through, but that's all part of the story, for the gift of music, the universal language, is that one encounters many tongues.

Nicky Gluch
London, 12 February 2019

'Blessed be the Lord, the God of Israel …
He will give light to those in darkness …
and guide us into the way of peace.'

The courtyard of St John of the Hills church in Ein Karem
where a prayer from the Book of Luke is written
in twenty-four languages.

Chapter 1: September

The regret I have is not writing this story when I was happy. Now I read back over the emails, with their joy and hope and spirit, and wonder where I've become lost in the intervening years. In the paper age, we sent off our thoughts. All we could keep were the replies, which broken hearts soon burnt. Now we have this trace of ourselves, a truth which tarnishes memory, with the replies embedded so that we cannot destroy one without the other. Besides, there is a limited catharsis in deleting files. I know.

Why then did I print this correspondence? Was it pride? Glory, perhaps? Or hope? But there it has sat in my drawer, the white pages bound by the rusting clip. The tiny font makes it uninviting, but I can't let that be an excuse. I must try.

The story opens in Helsinki. I was nineteen. Sitting in the airport, I wrote home about my travels, Dad and I having flitted from Berlin to the Finnish countryside.

We'd rowed, bathed in a sauna and cooked fish in a cabin with a fire alarm above the stove. It was idealised impracticality which I was desperate to set down, to capture, before the 'true' adventure began. My being there was contingent on my final destination, a decision made a year earlier to flee Sydney for a winter in Jerusalem.

The humour was in my lack of interest in Israel. I was home amongst the Finnish *pulla* and endless coffee. The German beer and concerts in the rain. I was unsettled by the idea of homelands, even more with becoming a cliché, and foolishly believed that I could go to Israel with a purely academic justification. It doesn't work like that. No country that has fought for its survival will not try and claim you as its own.

My flight to Israel was by way of Copenhagen, where I hurried past the restaurants, with their bread and caviar, to the security counter. A year before, I'd been stuck with eight other Aussies in Hong Kong airport. We'd taken the escalators, up and down, only to realise that the terminal was on some unreachable mezzanine. Detained, my countrymen cursed the Jewish State while I had to out myself as Jewish. What would we have done if I had not spoken Hebrew to the El Al officials with their music stand? We infiltrators with science degrees hoping to attend a camp on distant shores …

Personally, I was more terrified of the uniformed guards that now stood before me at Danish border control. I cowered at their questions and showed them the visa I shouldn't have had, since the Israeli embassies were closed due to an international strike. But some angel in Canberra had handled mine unofficially, and so I was let through to a silent gate. Men prayed all around me – some with mats and others upright with books. I sat, laptop on knees, and finished my story, longing for that bread I'd seen back behind security, for in this airport purgatory there was only a 7-Eleven store. Perhaps the men were praying for manna from heaven?

People who move to Israel do not say they immigrated. Rather they *alah,* ascend. My perception of Israel's airport is thus of happy families, or groups of friends, with celebratory balloons and open arms. It is a strange place to arrive to, alone. I headed to the exit, just behind the man who'd sat across from me on the plane. He turned towards the station and I thought of running to catch up, asking for his assistance, but instead joined the hoard waiting for taxis, disappointed by my lack of courage. So much for adventure!

Ascension, however, does strange things to reality. It elevates even the most mundane, so that a queue in Israel is not a queue, or so I learnt as each *sherut[1]* filled up without me. Laden with luggage and six passengers they pulled away, no room for me, the tourist wanting to go where the locals did not. And so I waited while the sun dipped lower, hunger growing alongside an element of fear. At last the crowds thinned and a driver had no reason to turn me down. I climbed aboard, and waited. A young Canadian got on and slumped against the window, and then there was a lull. Through the window I spotted a man and woman who were unmistakably military but, misled by their blond hair, I guessed they were Russian. I watched as they gestured to the driver to load their bags, and then climbed on, the woman's manner doing nothing to dissuade me of their supposed heritage. Until her companion spoke.

[1]Short for *monit sherut* or service taxi, a *sherut* is a form of ride share providing a point-to-point service for people heading to or from the airport.

'Hi, I'm Jim,' he boomed, hand outstretched. I shook it, introducing myself. An American! I was surprised by how quickly he made himself familiar. So they weren't a couple. Jim shook hands with the Canadian, Brock, and then tried to do so with a young religious woman who'd just got on. She politely explained his transgression. Another young man boarded and, full, we set off.

I have never been driven from the airport to Jerusalem in the daylight. I still do not know what the foothills look like, or how one gets there, just that the roads wind and that in places there is a strong sulphur smell. Jim chatted throughout the journey. Brock told him how he'd confused him, 'Coming in with that girl, and then chatting to that one, like, who're you *with*, Dude?' After which Brock threw up in his hat. And still we climbed.

Sandy, Jim's companion, said nothing. I took note. We turned off the road, dropped off the religious woman and then the young man. Back on the road we were welcomed into Jerusalem by letters mounted on a hill, 'Blessed comings,' to the city of peace.[2] Down lanes and alleys we drove and then the car – stopped. My suitcase was taken out and I was similarly instructed. Fear swept over me, as I recognised nothing of a place I knew that I'd been to before. I pulled the suitcase, tripping over cobblestones, hands shaking, breath shallow. What was I doing here? I could still go back to Helsinki, meet Dad, fly home. Instead I rounded the corner, found the hostel, then

---

[2]In Hebrew one is welcomed by the words *baruch habah* (or *bruchim habaim* in the plural). The direct translation is blessed comings. In both Arabic and Hebrew *salem*, in Jerusalem, is the root of the word for peace.

the dorm, and sulkily shoved my suitcase under my dorm bed. Back downstairs, I pocketed a brochure for the Chamber Music Festival, something to set aside for another day.

I was woken early in the morning by a woman drying her hair. Bleary-eyed, I got ready, put on my dress with the roses and polka dots that was to become my roommate's favourite. Hair in a clip, sunglasses on, I set out, into the overwhelming heat. Back over the cobblestones to King George's junction. Up onto the Egged bus[3], suitcase bashing my shins. Out into the sunlight of Mount Scopus, pulling my suitcase down the endless drive, soaked in sweat. By December I would laugh that this ever felt a long distance.

Into the University foyer, the aircon an abrasion to my skin.

'Hello,' boomed the voice. 'Would you look at that!'

A familiar chuckle. Jim and Sandy stood before me, he speaking for them both once more. He remarked on the odds of us meeting there. When I turned up in his apartment an hour later, he teased me that I was stalking him. I asked them about their night and agreed that, if we'd known, I might have come with them to their hostel then. After taking my leave, I went to sit my Hebrew exam. Ten minutes later, a man walked in – the same fellow who had sat across from me on the plane. After the girl I'd travelled with to the dorms turned out to be the only other in my class, I started to realise that coincidence was not just a word in Israel. It was a way of being.

---

[3]The Egged Cooperative is the largest transportation operator in Israel. Their green buses are in many ways a symbol of the country.

***

Student village, Mount Scopus. More poetically known as *Har Hatzofim*.[4]

The apartment was tiled and white, showing up the dirt. In the corner of the front room was a blue couch and a low coffee table. A dining table, also white, sat adjacent with its six wooden chairs. Later, I'd paper the walls with music, captured in photos of the five of us, and the chairs would be filled with friends. Lovers would meet at that dining table and the world's problems would be solved on the low blue couch. But the emptiness smugly kept this secret.

Jim's voice boomed around the corner. I'd ceased to be surprised.

On the *sherut* I'd learnt that Jim was from Michigan and would be entering the army 'next fall'. I came to know of his singing voice and hallway push-ups, belt-buckle clanging on the floor. The latter must have been contagious, for Robert, who roomed next to him, has since joined the service. There was a palpable sadness in Robert, manifested in a way that made me somewhat uneasy. I think, now, that he was searching for order. That's why he'd spent the summer working in a Sheriff's office. But to the world, Robert was simply a Texan. He liked *salsa* and beer and had no interest in being in Israel.

---

[4]*Me'al Pisgat Har Hatzofim* is the title of a song with lyrics by Avigdor Hameiri. So whenever I hear the words, I am reminded of the beautiful lilting melody to which it is set.

Robert had planned to learn Arabic in Egypt but others had planned a coup, so he found himself north of Sinai. Same story for Lucien, from Florida. Observing his dark-skin and thick-black hair, I was suddenly acutely aware that I'd never lived with men. There was a bomb shelter room in every apartment and fortune had blessed us in giving it to Luc. Of mixed Portuguese and French origin, he befriended the few Europeans on our program. Closing tight the stainless-steel outer door, they'd slip away into his sanctuary. Room for two, or three!

The last room belonged to Leanora, Lea-nora, for her two grandmothers, a most tender but anguished soul. We had no secrets, and why would we when the wall between us was like paper. But though I loved her, I could never pin her down.

'You know, for the first few days I couldn't understand you,' she told me once. 'I just nodded my head in pretend.' I looked through her to the wall shared by the neighbouring apartment. Four Aussies there, and I stuck here: unintelligible, bohemian, striving for an independence that wasn't synonymous with plastic plates and rotting onions. I shed bitter tears until coincidence reminded me that I would have been there if so intended.

Hebrew is a resuscitated language and all who study in Israel must give it breath. So our first few weeks were filled with strained expirations. In classes by aptitude, Leanora and I parted ways each morning, crossing paths again in the midday sun. 'I have this friend who lives on a kibbutz,' she said one day. Embedded in the statement, a question, 'Would I like to accompany her?' I was shy only of the fact that I knew this woman to be her lover but, not one to give up on an opportunity, set off with her in the heat of the afternoon. Down the hill to the tram stop. Past the Old City to the Central Station, aboard the Egged Bus bound for Kibbutz Gezer. Coincidence whispered, 'Your aunt's old home.'

For me as a child, Israel had simply been where Aunt Jo lived. I thought all the land a kibbutz. As a pre-schooler, I sang songs and drank orange-juice to celebrate Israel's 50th year. When I was five, Jo moved to Sydney, a photo of her milking cows tacked onto her apartment wall. I grew older, and Israel became a land of terror. I overheard adults' conversations – their fear for relatives, as people on buses or in cafes became bombs. Time passed. Jo stopped speaking Hebrew; I switched from it to French. My religion became a private matter, my connection to the Jewish community more tentative with each passing year. So at eighteen, my parents sent me to Israel. It was time I met some Jews. True, I fell in love with the desert. But for the rest, with all its divisions, I swore I'd never return.

The bus pulled up at our junction. My oath, broken twice.

Kibbutz Gezer welcomed us, the aged sign with its fading tomato. Odd, for Gezer means carrot. I remember that but not much else from the afternoon. Everything is blurred by the remarkableness of where we ended up; fragmented pictures come back, most of them in shades of brown. Somewhere in my story, Leanora's friend, I'll call her Sarah, comes into focus. I remember the tour she gave us, a view into a crumbling society. The gardens unkempt, the milking shed old and worn,

Marxism failed. First came the demise of the *Beit Yeladim* (Children's House) – parents restoring the idea of the family unit, choosing love over being pure 'comrades'. Capitalism had been the fatal blow. I've seen one kibbutz still thriving. Run by Americans, their product: tanks. I almost threw up on their posh auditorium floor.

In 1982, Amos Oz had his character bemoan, 'exile which masquerades as a rich uncle'. I saw that the charade had not declined in thirty years as Sarah led us past the baseball diamond where she and Leanora had met. Lush green from the greenbacks that funded it.

From the field, we headed towards Sarah's house. Our guide waved towards her parents and shouted out that I was Jo's niece. They smiled with recognition. Arriving in her home, Sarah excused herself. Leanora sat on the couch while I looked at all the pictures tacked onto the lounge room wall. Why was Jo's face staring back at me?

I remarked as much to Sarah upon her return. She shrugged her shoulders. 'Didn't you know,' she said, 'that this was Jo's house?'

Perhaps we ate. Perhaps Sarah escorted me back down the drive. Back on the Egged bus to Jerusalem. Back on the tram as the sun set towards evening. To my room, where I called Jo and left her a breathless message.

And so the weeks continued. I learnt Hebrew once more, tinged though it was by a French accent. We sang songs in our lessons and, come winter, I'd eat fresh oranges from the tree. On the blue couch, the boys learnt to read the letters. At the white dining table, they practised phrases over breakfast. I helped them with their pronunciation until the term started and *aleph bet* was replaced by *alif ba*[5].

***

In Israel, the year starts in Tishrei.[6] New year for humankind, but not for the earth – that's spring. My calendar now had two sets of dates, the week started on a Sunday and on each Friday was written that crucial thing: what time candles were to be lit, ushering in the Sabbath and ending the working week. Half useless, unless you knew that buses stopped some time before.

Class was cancelled, that last day of 5773. It was a Wednesday. Like the Sabbath, Jewish festivals start at sundown and so the two-day festival would lead us right in to Shabbat. There was a lot to prepare. My roommates, meanwhile, were looking forward to a three-day holiday. They'd partied the night away, perhaps not realising that vodka alone would not sustain them till Saturday night. Stocking-up was ruled out by their hang-over and on Thursday they were forced to venture to where the shops were open: in the Arab villages below. Imagine a society where three faiths live together, each with

---

[5] *Aleph bet* and *alif ba* are the first two letters of the Hebrew and Arabic alphabets, respectively. The first two letters of the Greek alphabet, *alpha* and *beta* are just another permutation.

[6] The Hebrew calendar has 12 months, alternating between 29 and 30 days in length. The civil year begins in *Tishrei*, said to mark the creation of Adam and Eve, whereas the religious year begins in *Nisan*, when the earth shows new life

their own day of rest. It should be so wonderful, so ...

I had no such choice. Though I am not *Shomrei Shabbat*, a keeper of the Sabbath, my family elevate the days known as the 'High Holy'. We do not drive, or use our phones, nor anything else electrical. In Sydney, we pause in a bustling society. What would it be like to rest in one that rests with you?

God said: 'Think not of it. Did I rest before my work was done?'

I replied: 'I bought the *challah*[7], already, while on my morning run. Did you not have the power to put pavements in your city,' I asked, 'that I must run in circles?'

And God, in whom I did not believe, replied: 'You just wait and see.'

I would, later, but I ignored the voice and rushed out to meet Sandy, friends since we'd ended up in the same *ulpan*[8] class, on the path between our buildings. It was the first of a trip that would become our ritual. The tram became more crowded at each stop. Mothers with prams. Young children darting between the few seats. Heaving up the hill past the Old City, slowing on the flat past the Ethiopian shops, finally to unburden at Machane Yehuda Market, known, simply, as 'The Shuk'.

<u>When I'd first come</u> to Israel, we'd travelled by coach. Illegal-

[7]In Ashkenazi tradition, a plaited white bread, enriched with egg and sugar, baked for the Sabbath and festivals.
[8]*Ulpan:* a school for the intensive study of Hebrew, the word meaning 'studio'.

ly parked, we'd get off and with our measured time, explore the market from its southern side. Lolly shops confronted us, sweet pastries and all sorts of tourist delights. We were somewhere that went beyond 'Israel' and yet was its lifeblood so to me the *shuk* was a heaven, overwhelmingly wonderful, and time always ran out before I could make sense of it.

On my second trip, I ventured deeper, off the main sunlit alley and into a vegetable grotto. All around me were shades of green; the prices marked, in chalk, on slate. I tried to buy a solitary cucumber but the vendor would have nothing of it – he gave it as a gift – and then found my way back into the sunlight and back to the group. I took them, then, for *shawarma*, proud to know a hole in the wall. But I was still a tourist, still staying on that southern side.

On the last day of 5773, I entered from the northern. 'Rimonim, rimonim, rimonim,' rang a vendor. Pomegranates for the new year. Tables were piled with apples, fresh dates, the seasons alive in the courtyard. From side to side voices called out, our bodies moved by the crowd as people searched for the best price. Sandy and I left the crush, disappearing into a dry-goods store. Bags of oats, rice, grain, sold by the kilo. I scooped some lentils into a plastic bag.

A leek, for the new year, and carrots too. Where once each culture had their own traditions, Israel has seen these collide. Polish apples meet Iranian dates and leeks, from France, perhaps. Down Fish Lane we went, as women bought heads for their table, and into the perfumed spice world. We guessed at the coloured powders but the variety was greater than we knew names. Yellow into one bag, red in another, Sandy wisely scribbling her choices in a notebook. Not I; this was the danger I lived by.

Sacramental wine into my backpack. Candles, too. A check of the time, and, I had to be off! The Chamber Music brochure had become worn in the intervening weeks but I had not forgotten it. 5774 would be heralded with music.

Laden with bags, I disembarked at City Hall. The tramline bends there, off Jaffa Road to hug the side of the Old City before heading into the hills. Over time, we would learn the names of each stop, reciting with the automated voice in three languages, but in early September each still felt like its own world.

City Hall was all about sandstone, and ice-cream vendors with special contraptions to yield the pomegranates' juice. I bought a bottle of sparkling water. The hydration was welcome, but I soon bought another, for the glass. Two bottles, with their thin necks and rounding forms to use as candlesticks.

In Sydney, we are used to streets named for kings and queens. New Jerusalem evokes that British world but the Old City pays tribute to its own. I walked down King Solomon Street, looking for his father, David. Sweat gathered behind my backpack and made my map useless. A wrong turn and I found myself on Abraham Lincoln Street, stern wall to one side, apartment buildings to the other, the road cracked beneath my feet.

Suddenly, a woman approached me. She looked as if she was

heading for the concert and I was about to ask for help when, in Hebrew, she asked me: do you know where the 'imkah' is? No, I replied, not even sure what she meant, and smiling, I hurried past.

I'd found myself on the map and began to make a beeline for the YMCA when it clicked. I turned, rushed back, and told the woman to follow me. In Jerusalem, the YMCA was dreamt up as a haven of interfaith – Hebrew resolves this by abstracting the Christian, an initialism becoming a two-syllable word, im-kah, a YMCA like nowhere else.

Peace is written in the tiles. It soothes in the water of the fountain. Opened in the year of Hitler's Nuremberg Laws, the YMCA was to serve a purpose undone by history. After the Holocaust, the gorgeous chambers became meeting rooms, while the UN tried to work out what to do for the State. Seventy years later, after so much pain and anguish, it has returned to its former purpose – pleading graciously for conciliation.

I found my seat in the concert hall in the midst of red velvet, only to find a man already there. Stressed, I tried to reason but he said simply: go get another. The ticket lady shrugged and gave me the number of another previously assigned seat; I thought of the absurdity of this ongoing cycle. 'Nu' she would have said to me, the man in my seat, too. You should be so lucky as to worry about these things.

All around me was an energy. People who'd rushed in, from shopping, from cleaning, who'd have to rush off once more, had chosen to press pause on this ultimate day. The MC entered, as sweaty as the rest, and his words spilled over in excitement.

When the music started, the air stilled, but stayed electric. Strains of Hindemith rang out, the composer I'd learnt to love most recently. Then Schumann, then a Mendelssohn Quintet. Musicians had gathered, laying down their ensemble allegiances and soloist reputations, to make music in combinations that existed only in that moment.

The climax was Mendelssohn's String Octet, that genius work for two conversing quartets. The domes of the YMCA hung on to every note, remembering how such things can happen, so that we could be reminded once the music ceased. We all rushed out, back to our preparations, back to our homes, too busy for an encore though utterly moved. Before that bugle sounded, before the sun set and so began a new year.

And when the year brought more pain and anguish, the YMCA would shed its tears. But the fountain would keep flowing, the tiles calming and the domes ringing true with music: that universal language which calls for peace.

Chapter 2: *Tishrei*

Numbers and letters swirl in Hebrew. Each letter has a numeric value so that words can be read as sums, codes analysed, meaning sought. 5774 thus becomes *tshad*: 400+300+70+4, or, reading the words now formed, *teisha + d*: 9+4 =13.

The number of fate and faith.

Those who know such things hoped it was a symbol of peace. They found the bible verse that corresponded, the prophet's voice which did declare:

And I will appoint a place for My people Israel, and will plant them, that they may dwell in their own place, and be disquieted no more; neither shall the children of wickedness afflict them anymore, as at the first. [9]

And so the children of the prophet prayed for his words to become truth. But I, while praying, began to ask, 'Who is Israel?' And was it the same as the world chooses to see? Rather than a singular perception of 'Israelis', I was starting to see a diversity.

---

[9]Samuel II 7:10.

Thursday morning: Happy new year.

I woke, later than planned. A metal grate on my window shut out the light and, in a city of cats, there were no birds to cheep, 'Good morning'. Turning in bed, I thought about the night before. The chaos of the communal dinner, I there, why, because my mum needed reassuring I wouldn't be alone. But she hadn't had to put up with the man buzzing round taking photos, or the woman who led the service in hippy garb and deemed the blessings 'too long to say'. Yes, I was bitter! But I would never let on. I'd laugh – one can with hindsight – and focus on the pleasure of talking religion with Sandy and a British girl long into the night. Standing there, in the foyer, the lift door opening and closing automatically … up and down, and up and down, Man's way of beating the strictures of the festival … thou shalt not create nor destroy, unless thou have an automatic timer. It was time to get up.

Pita and water for breakfast, before slipping outside, my key and ID card in my glasses case. 'Good morning,' I said to the security guard. '*Boker tov*,' he smiled in reply, as I left through the glass door, and turned right out of the complex, towards where I knew there to be a *shul*. [10]

There it was, behind the supermarket; everything in dirty sandstone, broken signs pointing to the ceremonial baths. Around, and around, I walked, trying to find an entrance. No people about, but song coming from within. I followed it, found a door that opened and climbed narrow stairs to the women's gallery. A narrow balcony with narrow pews. '*Boker*

---

[10]Yiddish for synagogue.

tov,' I said to the women with dark skin and scarf-covered hair. They replied with their eyes. I took a seat, hoping it was not another's place, and searched in the all-Hebrew prayer book for where we seemed to be. But the *chazan* [11] was barely audible from the men's section down below. To not be different, I thought, is why I came to Israel.

I stood when the women did. Sat too. They were devout in their practice, sincere. Until … rowdiness broke out. An auction had begun! Straining to hear what was happening, I eventually caught on.

Each reading from the Torah is divided into sections, five for a weekday festival, seven for Shabbat. Men, in Orthodoxy, or women, can be honoured with a portion. Blessings to them, and, in return, money for the community. In the West, a congregant is chosen; it would be improper to say no, though synagogues are conscious of those without means. Where I was seated, however, the true tradition bore on: each honour was bargained for, and bestowed, finally, on the highest bidder.

Later, I would understand why, but at first I marvelled that the women joined in. Dissatisfied with their husband's price, they would bid on their behalf, old bodies leaning over rails and shouting out in clear voice: '300 *shekel*, 400 *shekel*'. *Beseder*, OK.

They were not alone in raising voice. From the Torah, we learnt how Sarah, barren, had asked God for a child.

---

[11]Cantor.

And so Isaac came to be born. Time ticked on … from the book of prophets, Hannah gave up her cry. 'Remember me, oh God.' And from her loins sprang Samuel. From Isaac came the Jewish people, and from his brother Ishmael, the Arab world. And Samuel? He would come to speak the words of our year: *And I will appoint a place*…

Faith, and fate, a hope for peace. Is that what calls out when the *shofar* [12] is blown? Imagine a bell ringing every morning in December, preparing you, warning you, that judgement is to come. And then, on New Year's day, you gather as that bell rings one hundred times. I was shaken from my tradition, as the *shofar* blasted the silent prayer. In Eastern Europe, a fear crept through that we had to order things so that we could not do wrong. So we have convinced ourselves that it is better to wait until the end of service before blowing these 30 blasts, while bodies droop and all do want for lunch … But now, in a penetrated silence, I understood the awe.

Silence, deeply praying, three steps back, bow left: *May He who makes peace on high places,* bow right, *make peace for us*, bow forward, *and for all Israel, and let us say, amen*, three steps forward. Silence ended.

The *chazan* began his recitation but we were too soon upon the Angel's Prayer. I flipped the pages, back and forth, until, finally, I realised what was missing. While the Jews were living in Spain in relative harmony, those in the East were suffering, and spurned.

---

[12] The ceremonial ram's horn.

In the 13th century, a rabbi in Mainz, tortured, dying, pulled himself up to the altar and, just before the Angels, gave his own supplication.

We Ashkenazi Jews have, and will, recite his words for ever more. *Unetaneh Tokef,* [13] a wail that shakes me to the core. The prayer's absence, and I felt it, explained the women's dark skin and their wonderfully vocal attitude. I had entered through the wrong door! I was amongst Spanish descendants, Sephardim.

The next day, I would find the Ashkenazi building where the women were pale and wore wigs to cover their hair. American voices twittered around me, but none would have dared bid for blessings. I slipped out, back to the world of headscarves hiding curls.

But that first day, when the service ended I wandered home for lentil soup and intimate conversation. Leanora told me of her life and we shared stories of how we came to be there. I rested in the afternoon, while she sang songs and strummed on her guitar. As evening came, we set out on the long walk to the Old City. At the Western Wall was a pulsating mass of people and, in front of it, we became the subjects of our own auction: bids for dinner places.

'I have two girls here,' called Jeremy, the auctioneer. 'Anyone take two lovely girls? Or three boys, good boys from the US? Anyone, anyone?'

---

[13]Let us cede power.

Jeremy Moses was short in a way that made him seem eternally childlike. He wore sneakers with his suit, a cap instead of a *kippah* [14] and disarmed enough influential Americans to run a student centre that nourished and stimulated any youth who entered it. He was also a baseball fanatic and so had taken to Leanora, the softball champion, on first meeting. She was the anointed one, his guest for the evening, and I the one Jeremy kept asking: 'What's your name again?'

Jeremy led us through the alleys of the Old City, off the tourist drag and down tiny lanes we would never find in the morning. Leanora whispered in my ear: 'I never imagined that people actually lived here!' Israelis did, then they didn't, now Americans do … but we had so much more to discover.

At the door, we were met by Jeremy's wife and his equally small, though adult, children. Wine was poured, the blessing said. Hands washed, bread broken, and a toast made. The first, of many.

Each of the symbolic foods lay before us in small, plastic tubs. We followed the process, bless one, toast one, eat one… smaller and smaller sips as the wine did flow. *L'chaim!* To life! Leanora and Jeremy drunkenly chatted ball while his wife and I, more sober, switched recipes. Friends arrived, lone soldiers, and joined in the merriment. With a final glass of wine, Leanora and I took our leave. We were bold, stumbling out of the labyrinth, out onto Jaffa Road to begin our journey home.

It was late, or, rather, it was early, as we walked down qui-

---

[14]Skullcap.

et streets. 'Let's walk on the tram track,' Leanora suggested. And so we did. Arab youths drag-raced old cars in the streets. Cats darted in front of us, down into lanes where we'd been told never to go. But we kept walking north, down the metal line. And God whispered in my ear: 'Do you still miss the pavement?'

***

Rosh Hashanah is the day of judgement, but in God's court you have 10 days to appeal. Only on Yom Kippur, too simply known as the Day of Atonement, is one's fate sealed. On the festival's eve, all vows are annulled. One is unchained, unshackled, cast into the void of the unknown. That's why you have ten days to atone, to repent, to introspect, to throw breadcrumbs to fish, each morsel a sin, if you must … for you *must* right your wrongs.

In this period can fall only one Shabbat, the most important of the year. When Rosh Hashanah begins on a Thursday, as it did that year, it dovetails with Shabbat Shuva.[15] Not my preference, for I feel the day's weight is somehow lessened but to my hosts that Friday evening, the co-incidence was truly magical.

Leanora and I had arrived once more in front of the Western Wall. Rightwards and leftwards, we watched young girls sent off with strange men, but Jeremy promised us he'd saved us for the best. At last it was our turn, and we followed our stranger back down the Old City lanes.

---

[15]*Shuva* comes from *t'shuva* meaning repentance.

Ahead of us were three girls I half-recognised. One turned and whispered: 'He could be taking us anywhere,' and I rankled that she'd put the idea in my mind. At some point we stopped, opened a gate, climbed some stairs, a Filipino maid meeting us at the open door. Not using electricity means no doorbells. I loved it!

Out we were ushered, onto a balcony. Seated, we looked upon the Dome of the Rock. Did they know we were penniless students? I looked around at my friends' walking shoes, scruffy hair ... their reluctantly worn skirts. In my neatness, I stood out – all the less welcome, for not needing to be saved.

From guide, our strange man became inquisitor. 'What brought you to Israel?' We answered each in turn. I explained how in Sydney I'd studied medical science and had manoeuvred a way to spend six months in Jerusalem learning about the brain.

'Why?'

'I want to be a surgeon ...'

'I knew I liked you,' came a voice from across the table, my story interrupted.

She had a grin that made you smile back. Loud, tall, everything I wasn't. Tanya. And for a time we were great friends. But later, when I was struggling to find my own identity, I hurt her. Feeling crushed, misunderstood, I made her break her grasp. And once released, there was no going back. A sur-

geon needs a nurse. But a conductor, as I would become …
But not then. The thought had not entered my mind.

I smiled back, learning that she was from Tennessee, and more
and more as she talked infectiously. Shots rang out below, another Palestinian couple happily married … when before us
appeared our bride.[16] Rosanna, hostess, adorned in white with
flowing sleeves and a turban to cover her hair. 'Come my children,' she cooed, 'dinner is served.'

There we were in a palace, in a building a thousand-years-old.
Layer upon layer, inhabitant after inhabitant, banquets lain for
every cause. We took our seats at the table, dispersed amongst
Rosanna's friends. Holding hands we were the welcomed
ones on this sacred night, Israel's children, like the Israeli soldiers who were Rosanna's cause.

In contrast to her vibrancy, sat her husband, stolid, plain. His
name was Dod (Uncle). But whose? Ours, the soldiers, or
hers? It all became inseparable.

Before the blessings, we sang songs, American voices joining
in these Hebrew praises. A woman turned to me, 'You know
the tune.'

'Why yes,' I said, 'we sing it at my *shul*.'

'To what words,' she enquired.

---

[16]It is a strange thing to adjust to, that this sound, normally so ominous,
can also denote something celebratory.

How particular, I thought, but I told her.

'Yes, I suppose that might work,' she replied. And still I found it odd. They were tunes, carelessly thrown about by the person leading our service, changing with the mood and the season.

A man lent over and whispered in my ear, 'Her husband wrote that tune. Shlomo Carlebach, the great songwriter, that's his widow.'

I fretted. Had I been rude to Jewish royalty? But underneath that question, another one: was the world really that small?

The singing paused, the wine was blessed, then Rosanna swept up us girls to wash our hands in an ornate basin cut into the stone. It was a happy silence as we waited for the bread to be blessed – round challahs dipped in honey to sweeten the new year – and then the sound was turned up again as conversation spilled out.

The maid, and others from her country, passed round food on metal platters. Red hearts on white cloth, their t-shirts promoted Rosanna's organisation. Thank those who serve you. So I tried, but they didn't want my gratitude. And I couldn't decide whether it was my pacifism or socialism that made me more uncomfortable.

Thoughts ceased as I tasted the food. Rich eggplant, fragrant rice dishes, more and more each time I looked. I relaxed, drew out of the moment and took it all in. A spoon hit a crystal glass and order was called upon the table.

'We are so blessed to be here,' Rosanna intoned, 'each of us for our own reasons, on this special Shabbat, the first of the year. And now each of us shall tell why God put them here today. As you know, God found me, and I found Dod, and together we are so blessed to bring beautiful people into our home.'

The woman next to her stood up, and began her tale, then the man next to her, and round the table we began. They were repenters, *Ba'alei Teshuva*, here to show us the glory of the Orthodox path … so I, born onto it, removed their purpose.[17] But when Leanora spoke, well, all eyes were upon her. Passion and imperfect eloquence, one could not help but drink it up. She spoke in a way that revealed her soul and I thought of how I used words to hide mine.

Dinner flowed on, and on, singing, and talking, and eating. Drunk on good feelings and inspiring conversation. Eventually we made to take our leave. Leanora and I went to thank Rosanna, whose embrace was interrupted by an older, limping woman.

Rivkah grasped Leanora's hands. 'You remind me of me when I was young,' she said. 'I want you to read my book.' And with that she parted, no question that we would find her, or she us.

Again, we tried to go. 'Thank you Rosanna, it was lovely, but we really must be going.'

---

[17] Australian Jews are still predominantly Orthodox, unlike in America where the Liberal traditions rule.

'To the women's hostel?' she enquired.

No, we explained, back to the dorms, back to Har Hatzofim …

'You will not,' Rosanna declared. 'It is too dangerous. You shall stay with me.'

In her trail, we descended, the four American students and me. In a basement room lay five mattresses. A gown on each bed, and a toothbrush. We sat on the beds, knees to the side like young children, as Rosanna bent and kissed us each in turn.

When we could no longer hear her footfalls, we broke the silence, laughing, giggling, delirious and then exhausted. Unbelieving, we fell into a deep sleep.

It was after 10 the next morning before we emerged. In our dressing gowns, we padded up the stairs, nervous to find it all a dream. But on the balcony, now lit gloriously by the sun, were fresh fruit, pastries, an urn for tea and coffee. Repentance had never tasted so sweet.

***

Here, I must confess that as wonderful as it was to be in Jerusalem for the festivals, with the buses passing by wishing you a happy new year, the overwhelming feeling was relief that I was not in Sydney. University had been a shock after high school's false security. After being respected for my religious affiliation, aided by my school and my synagogue sharing a fence so that trust was not an issue, I had arrived at university as an adult, to have my religion questioned.

If you were an Arts student, it was less a problem. But for us scientists with compulsory laboratory time, needing to take off for the festivals was a nuisance exacerbated by computerised timetables, which removed any grey area necessary for negotiation.

And so the run-ins with staff began. The most memorable occurred in my third year when, the professor, having promised me exemption, changed his mind and decided that I should sit his exam the afternoon before it was scheduled. I politely emailed, explaining that Jewish festivals start at sundown, so that his suggested 3 pm would leave it too late for me to get home – to which he kindly replied telling me the time the sun set, in case I hadn't known it.

This was when my colleague stepped in, negotiating for the exam to start an hour earlier. And so we found ourselves standing in the neuroscience offices at 1:45 pm the next day, being asked by said professor if we kept the festivals by choice.

'Surprisingly enough, yes.'

Now this was a matter of religion, somewhat controversial in the modern world, but it didn't surprise me in the slightest, considering two years prior the science department had given me a hard time for wanting to represent the country in their very field.

One evening, my Dad had come downstairs, letter in hand.

'Do you want to go back to Israel?' he asked.

'No, why, what for?' I rudely replied, for it had only been four months earlier that I'd asserted I would never return, the country a mess, everyone fighting, everything false.

But then Dad told me that it was for a camp at the Hebrew University. We'd been there on the last day of my trip, I'd had a fever, indeed may have been slightly delirious, and so upon seeing this oasis of knowledge in a desert of despair, thought it one of the most beautiful places I had ever been. For the chance of returning, I applied and, as is relevant to this story, became a science delegate by sending in a music composition.

(A matter of humour … the camp turned out to be in Givat Ram, the campus built after the 1948 war when Israel lost access to Mount Scopus and not, therefore, on the campus I had visited. But I have been forever grateful for my oversight.)

There was, however, a slight problem. The camp was in the northern hemisphere summer, so I'd have to miss a week of class, but as the Engineering Faculty proudly displayed banners of their students who were to represent Australia at the Olympics, it wouldn't be a problem, right?

'You'll have to catch up,' wrote one professor.

'You'll miss your test,' wrote another.

Pity, I thought, that I'll be learning from Nobel scientists.

I caught up, I forfeited the test, and I came back happier than I'd been for a long time. One student snidely remarked on it, 'You're back at uni, so why do you look so pleased?'

I would have told her: of the marvel of meeting 350 young scientists from around the globe, of learning, and touring, and eating and playing cards long into the night so that we were drifting off as yet another genius shared their wisdom, and blushing, but not caring, because *we* were young … But she didn't want to hear.

I had lifted the lid on the fact that there was a world outside our esteemed establishment.

Poor Prometheus.

Surprisingly, my university in Sydney was not encouraging about my desire to return to Israel to learn more from the world-class neuroscience facility. I went from department to department, hoping someone might recognise a course in Jerusalem as equivalent to their own … but my form stayed unsigned. Finally, a professor in the maths department relented. A compromise: one of his courses for the equivalent of three in Jerusalem. But no firm guarantee …

This was the saga I regaled my academic advisor, a Scotsman, with on our first meeting, somewhere in the ten days between Rosh Hashanah and Yom Kippur.

I appreciated his Commonwealth sense of humour and his Jewish piety dressed in plain clothes. He looked at me, bemused, and said quite simply,

'So why did you fight so hard?'

He was a philosopher, so the question could only be answered by another.

'You mean, what am I here to achieve?'

I then told him that I would need his help in answering that question. I was in his office to petition taking his course. No, I had no prior knowledge. At least, not the kind certified by a university.

'Philosophy?'

'No.'

'Criticism?'

'No.'

'Religion?'

'No… it's more like physiology, chemistry and r…'

'Alright,' he interrupted, 'you're here to study the brain so you might as well learn to use it.'

I smiled and started to thank him when he interjected again.

'But I'm warning you, I'm saying this only as your teacher, not as your advisor.'

That made me smile all the more. The threat excited me and, buoyant on my bravado and the repartee, I left.

When I woke, it was Friday, the eve of Yom Kippur. Back down the hill we went to the *shuk*, back on the crowded tram, back down the crushing aisles. Imagine, at nineteen, experiencing your first 'Christmas Eve'.

I had promised to bring tiramisu to the post-fast meal but had to improvise for want of a whisk. The poor Americans suggested I beat the eggs with a fork (I opted instead for the electric chopper). Leanora beat the mascarpone into such submission that it became a liquid mess and we all got drunk on the coffee liqueur I'd bought to soak the biscuits.

At sundown, we put food and water to one side and I headed to *shul* to bear witness to Kol Nidrei. Perhaps the most stirringly performed legal tractate in all of history …

All vows we are likely to make, all oaths and pledges we are likely to take between this Yom Kippur and the next Yom Kippur, we publicly renounce …

Saturday, standing, we prayed. That day we knelt to pray[18] – the cloth from my glasses case all I had to cover the stone

---

[18]In the Jewish tradition, kneeling is not a part of the normal prayer service. On *Rosh Hashanah* we kneel once but it is only on *Yom Kippur* that we kneel repeatedly.

floor. We rested in the afternoon, returning in the evening, when the heat had risen in the women's gallery. Dripping with sweat, we stood at the window, hoping that some breeze might save us, pounding our chests with our right hands in apology.

There were no cars on the streets. Silence, even in the Arab villages below. And after twenty-five hours, when that *shofar* blasted, we all sang with joy, with an energy that comes as if from nowhere, and we hugged and kissed the strangers beside us. I thought, *I'm beginning to know why I've come.*

.

Chapter 3: October

There was nothing like *Sukkot* in Jerusalem. Not the festival itself. That was essentially familiar and the story of the dinner I attended is too filled with rancour to tell here. No, what was unique was the festival's presence; the way the *sukkot* (sing. sukkah) transformed every street, every cramped balcony so that for a week, the city had a new vista. A *sukkah* is a hut and by design it is impermanent. (It is also a rude word in Russian and thus the cause of many a giggle when I was in high school.) Atop the walls must go a roof of natural product, palm leaves, by tradition, or a bamboo mat in our now East-meets-West world. Let the heavens reach us, that we be reminded both of our vulnerability and God's protection.

In Israel, the rains do not fall until winter and so these autumnal dwellings provide a form of shade. Whereas in Sydney's springtime, we often have to wrap ourselves in blankets, or run inside when a drizzle turns to downpour – but it's as much a part of the tradition as the paper chain decorations.

As a child, I'd wished each year for my own hut. But there was always a reason why not: the fabric was too expensive, the garden too small, the maple-tree too low. 'Maybe next year,' my Dad would say. Eventually I resigned myself to this, burdened with wondering if I had wanted one for the novelty or to fulfil the sense that we were not doing things 'right'.

Perhaps that's why I was so struck by the situation in Jerusalem – in a city of obligation, there was no excuse but to build in whatever permissible space existed, so the number of inhabitable dwellings in Jerusalem almost doubled. It made me wonder how similar historic cities would have been transformed. *Shtetls* in Poland, Spanish towns before the Inquisition …

If not for the trip we took in the holiday week, I may not have been aware of any of this. The student village was on an isolated peninsula and, before the official semester started, I had little cause to travel beyond the city centre. It was on the day after the festival, however, as we returned by bus from the train station, and before the *sukkahs* had been dismounted, that I became witness to what would become one of my favourite scenes.

The two festival days of *Sukkot* bound a week of semi-holiday and we students had been blessed with a vacation. Keen to explore the country, Sandy, Leanora, Tanya, two of their friends and I headed north on a roughly planned trip filled with competing expectations. Being the most fluent in Hebrew, it had been my responsibility to make the hostel bookings, calling the proprietors in the break during *ulpan*, details scribbled in my diary. With no written confirmations, it was a good test of faith.

We arrived in Haifa on a Friday afternoon. No *sukkahs* there in the predominantly Arab city centre. Though it was for this reason that we planned to be there on *Shabbat*, we had forgotten to consider the converse effect this would have on Friday: it was *salaat al-jumu'ah* and the town was, in effect, shut. Grumbling was soon replaced by hunger and we found somewhere suitably touristy to dine. What the rest of us ate, I have long forgotten, for Tanya's *shakshuka*, with its thick tomato sauce and perfectly baked, still-runny eggs, deserves its distinction.

When evening came, we dined on Ben-Gurion Boulevard and I had to concede that it was as complicated travelling with Jews as *goyim*, for guilt grips me on any *Shabbat* that I do not mark. My Dad and I had blessed cider and barley porridge in our Finnish cabin and I have since created unique experiences across the globe. Ironically, it was to a Haifa Jew that I recently explained my own version of affiliation: *chezi-chezi*, half-half. Half the rules kept, or rules kept to half their extent, but as they're kept, it pains me to break them.

Saturday morning was glorious and we decided on a hike. From our hostel, the Line 1 bus (*chezi-chezi* like me, it runs on *Shabbat* but is free and waits at each stop, so as not to offend Observant sentiment) snaked through the suburbs to the coast where the Carmel beach lay at the base of the same-named mountain. Leaving the ocean for the evening, we followed the guidebook to the old, though not ancient, cemetery and, after a few wrong turns, celebrated our triumph upon finding the entrance.

'This weirds me out,' said one of us. We all agreed. The sun shone on the white tombstones while, before us, the shade of the rocky path beckoned. In single file we began our ascent. We learnt about each other as we walked: how Sandy's army training shaped her walk, how Tanya's car accident strained what had always been an athletic body and how Leanora's friend Claire, poor Claire, pushed on despite her genetic illness. At some points we stopped and looked at the splendid view, at others we smiled upon children splashing in the natural pools.

We were on one side of a ravine. To our left was the mirror hill, capped by a mosque from which descended a stone staircase.

'Could we not go down that way?' Claire suggested.

'Let's try,' I replied. A mistake!

But first we had to reach the summit. Sweating, we climbed, further and further, as rock became soft leaves. Then, as abruptly as it had begun, the path ended and we found ourselves in the Jewish suburbs. With a slight embarrassment as to our attire, we turned left.

Where the walk had been our equaliser, back in the city we were six individuals, competing for our needs once more. Hunger, thirst, money, short tempers … each eventually sorted out in turn. Not quite replenished, we headed towards the mosque. Around it and around it we went, but no path made itself apparent. The staircase loomed before us, two metres from our grasp. In different circumstances, I might have ambled down the dirt passage (I know Sandy would have for sure) but stray cats hissed their reproach and so, not feeling quite brave enough, I admitted defeat, 'Sorry Claire, but I've led you astray.'

Her face made it clear that she was in too much pain to walk. The bus signs were equally sure that we were without an option until evening. And then, as if by magic, a taxi appeared. Four of them bundled in, leaving Sandy and me alone. Through the taxi window we called out, 'We'll meet you at Carmel beach.'

As I looked out for another cab, Sandy asked, 'Do you mind if we walk?'

Between the lines, I realised she did not want to pay so I assented. I was fit back then; it was two years before I became ill. So, back down the path we went, as I glared at the stone staircase, a mystery unsolved. We spoke, we shared, and it was this walk that in many ways secured our friendship. Without lingering, we passed the splashing children. With relief, we arrived back at the cemetery as a message came through on my mobile: Are you almost here?

About to reply in the affirmative, the beach hotels looming before me, I suddenly realised that we were on the wrong side of the highway. Cars flashed past, heading towards the city, those headed to the beach separated from us by a high metal fence. I'd had enough!

Legs weary, phone still going: 'How long will you be?' Sandy and I set off towards the junction. I suppose my silence was frosty for it was not long before she said, 'You know what we do in the army when we need perking up?'

I shrugged my soldiers.

'We sing cadence.'

From two-abreast, we re-arranged in single file, Sandy ahead teaching me the tunes, I responding in full voice.

And down the highway we marched, two young women singing bawdy songs, horns tooting, whistles blowing as the sun set on an unforgettable day.

***

The next few days were postcards of activity. On Sunday, when business reopened, we travelled to see Elijah's cave and then, for Sandy's sake, the Clandestine Immigration Museum. She'd sold it to us as a naval space and we'd thought 'How dull!' but the tales and trials of the Jews who'd fled Europe after Hitler's rise, and the way they'd sneaked into the country that was still not their own, fascinated us all. Suddenly the idea of Haifa as a port made more than nominal sense and the cemetery we'd walked through, established in this clandestine period, echoed with a new solemnity. The Holocaust memorials had been tributes to the families of these immigrants.

For the afternoon's activity, I had persuaded the group to visit the Druze village which had so fascinated me on my first trip to Israel. In the five weeks, it had been one of the few high-lights, as we'd been taken to a local's home and plied with delicacies (a joy after the cold meat sandwiches that were so often called lunch). Always fascinated by religion, I'd loved learning of this unique faith where men and women are considered equal and all members are thought reincarnates of ancestors. It is natural for outsiders to be drawn to the faith and therein lies the great wisdom of the Druze: they do not permit conversion.

On this trip, in our tourist guise, we were to be privy to no such information so I played teacher as we took the bus high into the Carmel mountains. Arriving in Daliyat el-Karmel we made short choice of a place for lunch, and ordered the banquet, notable for me who can rarely do such a thing. Plate upon plate of food arrived; dips and salads, bread and oily rice. We ate with gusto, and then more tentatively, as it occurred to us that this was only the first course. There was no space on the table when the meat and chips arrived and, graciously, our hosts offered to pack the leftovers away for our supper.

In the afternoon we explored the town but missed the bus back for having lost a group member. We found her in a teahouse, enjoying the plump Turkish delight, and the sweet humour of the scene made it too hard to chastise her. But, as appointed group leader, I firmly suggested Liat be early for the next bus, or we would not make it to our lodgings by nightfall.

Fifty minutes were well spent, peering into more antique stores and trying on the over-priced clothes. Leanora entertained us all when, needing the bathroom, she walked confidently into a café, asked '*Sherutim*?' mid-flight, and kept moving before the waiter suggested she might order anything. Five minutes later, the bus appeared, but now it was Claire who was missing for she'd taken a seat in the shade. I knew she couldn't run and so tried a different tack; as the bus pulled away, I jumped on and, rather hyperventilating, told the driver he had to wait. God knows why he did but for a moment I enjoyed being the hero!

As part of our northern adventure, we'd decided to spend a night on a kibbutz. Near the junction to Akko lay the Ghetto Fighters' Kibbutz: *Lohamei Ha'Getaot.* The name was the same as the street we lived on back in the student village. There, the transliterated Hebrew had done nothing to reveal that word, ghetto, hidden within.

Led by the proprietor of the B&B, we were shown to unexpectedly plush rooms. Showered and refreshed, we retrieved the stowed food from my backpack and, seated like girls at a slumber party, tucked in to a second feast. As an aside to this, it was with great alarm that I discovered that the grease had not stayed within the double layer plastic bag. I panicked, thinking my passport a write off, but fortunately my novel had martyred itself, absorbing every drop. That my passport was saved by Huxley's *After Many a Summer* (with its theme of mortality) is more apt than I could contrive.

The night was filled with conversation about sexual exploits, the morning with breakfast so sumptuous we made it count as lunch. Our luggage left in the office, we posed for photos in front of the amphitheatre and a 19th century aqueduct, before turning towards the 'Ghetto Fighters' House'. We had chosen the kibbutz for its location, ignorant to the idea we were at a site of history, for what lay before us was not just a Holocaust museum but the first in the world. It had been founded by survivors, in much the same way as the Museum in Sydney where I had worked for many years. But not in the 1990's, like our museum, rather, in 1949. The testimony least affected by time, perhaps?

It was many hours before we emerged. Dazed, we re-entered the sunshine. We'd been silent for so long, we didn't know what to say.

Reclaiming our bags, we got in the taxis ordered for us. Onwards to Akko, the experience lingering, not ready to be probed.

As unplanned as the museum visit had been, by contrast our arrival in Akko was considered. In being a weeklong festival, *Sukkot* is the perfect time for festivities and Akko holds a theatre fair. Road blockades made entering the town difficult, and as we were dropped outside the city gates we were spotted by the proprietor of our hostel. Six young women do not go unnoticed in an ancient town!

The man shouted directions at us from his bicycle, which we followed down labyrinth paths. Upon arriving at a peaceful two-story building, our hostess greeted us, dressed all in black, and showed us up to our brightly painted rooms. Four girls had single beds while I shared the double with Liat. The risqué poster pinned large above our heads became our secret.

Returning downstairs, I tried to ask the woman where we might find the bus the next day. With a cryptic smile she said, 'I'll tell you this evening. Now, do you have the money?'

I proffered my card but no, she only took cash, and never have I guarded money more closely than the 1200 *shekel* I withdrew for her that day. Money secured, she provided the requested information and, in doing so, taught us a crucial lesson: trust, here, was not a word.

But that was part of Akko's charm. Within the city walls, one entered into a different era. It was a pocket of the Ottoman Empire, at least seemingly undisturbed. Perhaps too gleefully, I sent my friends off to see the Rosh Hanikrah Grotto, while I explored the city, alone. On the square, men drank coffee, cigarettes burning next to backgammon boards. The covered market was filled with fruit, nuts and meat and wonderful spice pyramids: thyme, sumac and sesame mixed to make *za'atar.*

I wandered down many lanes while the hawkers set out their wares, before choosing a *hummus* shop for a late breakfast. Pita, hot; hummus, thick; raw onions, pickles, tomato, eaten with the hands; all washed down by water … it was a joy to eat with abandon.

The group returned, hot and bothered, and I felt a twang of guilt, comforted only by contemplating whether they would have seen the town with my eyes.

When the sun set, the entertainment began and street theatre acts appeared as if from nowhere. Crunching popcorn and toffee apples, we watched as a young woman played drums and grown men dressed as babies drank and spat out milk.

No photos will ever do justice to how happy I was.

All festivals, however, must come to an end and so on the seventh day of *Sukkot*, it was time to move on to Tsfat. The idea had been to be in this centre of mysticism for the special festival of *Simchat Torah*. In Judaism, the five books of Moses are read in an annual cycle. *Simchat Torah* is the day the cycle ends, and begins again. It is perhaps the most visceral day on the calendar as bodies are given over to dancing and singing, aided by whiskey, with religiously fuelled abandon.

What I had forgotten to consider, is that my travel mates were from the Reform and Liberal traditions. On seeing the men and women separated in the synagogues, they were so offended that we did not stay for more than ten minutes. As the trip began in grumbling, so it seemed it would end.

Believing there was 'nothing to do' the group slept in the morning, while I set out to explore. I returned, they hadn't stirred, so I set out again, this time accompanied by Liat who had similarly become bored. As we walked in aimless circles, we heard song coming from near the town hall. Following it, Liat and I walked into a *shul* we hadn't realised was there and, as if perfectly timed, heard the recitation of the last chapter, and then the first: *In the beginning, God created the Heaven and the Earth ...*

Our spirits raised, we returned to the downhearted group and for what in Hebrew we term *shalom bait*[19] I decided to forgo the festival strictures and organise a trip to a nearby village. In a taxi van, we travelled to Jish where we encountered the third Abrahamic faith. Just kilometres from Lebanon, Jish is a Maronite outpost and the gorgeous churches and non-kosher food somehow restored decorum. In more recent years, however, as the war in Syria has raged on and Middle Eastern Christians have found themselves so persecuted, I have thought back to that festive afternoon and understood why the first portion of the Torah, in which life comes to be, includes, as well, the first death. We are Cain and Abel, from generation unto generation …

In the evening we returned to Tsfat and waited for the sun to set and the weekday to begin. And it did, as it always does, but it was not a quiet evening. In the distance we heard music, loud, like at a rave and so, with nowhere to be, again we followed the sound.

The courtyard of the town hall had been transformed. Divided down the centre, men were on one side, women on the other and they were dancing, arms joined and feet moving one in front of the other. On what is the eve of Simchat Torah in the Jewish diaspora[20], Tsfat celebrates the festival for a second time. 'Why not?' they say, 'when this time we can have electricity, when the music can come over speakers, and fairy lights can illuminate the garden.'

---

[19]Peace in the home.
[20]The term for the places the Jewish people live, outside of Israel.

And so we danced, until we were thirsty, and then bought sodas from the vendor and danced some more. Back in Jerusalem, we learnt that the party had raged on until morning; we hadn't known it, sleeping soundly as we were in our hostel, happy, *sameach*, like the festival insists one should be.

***

Ulpan resumed on Sunday morning. For once we all had an answer to the teacher's opening question: what have you been up to? We just didn't have the words! The ethos of *ulpan* is that it is fully immersive; English was banned. Clarification came in the form of pictorial gestures and, when our brains couldn't retrieve a word, our teacher pointing to her ear, 'sounds like', and providing us with a sonic clue.

It was a genius system – if you gave in to it. Be tired, and the search for synonyms became too much. Be impatient, like the young man in my class, and you would entertain everyone. Sam was eighteen, though he looked older, and the only student from the UK. Exceedingly bright, he was bored with *ulpan*'s games and often had a stand-off with our softly spoken teacher, Margalit.

In Hebrew, his story would begin but then, chancing on a word he didn't know, Sam would slip in English without even the slightest pause. *B'Ivrit*[21], Margalit would request. So Sam would continue, until he became stuck again but, no matter, he'd just apply a Hebrew modifier and hope no-one would notice.

---

[21]In Hebrew.

'*Halachti ba'midbar, v'*climbed*ti el ha'har.*'[22]

We couldn't but laugh.

Day to day, our lives were pleasantly routine. Class began at nine with a short quiz to review the homework. We'd then practice conversation, or read a simple section from the news-paper, before embarking on the content for the day. I think many of my classmates were surprised by how little vocab we learnt directly. What they didn't realise was how much we picked up, passively, as the verbs and grammar we were instructed in helped the language take form.

Margalit's sweet temperament was balanced by the stead-fast charm of our other teacher, Roman. They played to their strengths, Margalit telling us stories and Roman grilling us in dictation. I admired them both. So used was I to their language fluency, it caught me by surprise when I realised that Margalit not only didn't speak English in class, but could not outside it. During semester, I saw her several times in the campus cafeteria. We smiled, but I would have loved to make more of her maternal presence.

It was during a morning 'conversation' session that Sam told me of his volunteering at Hadassah Hospital. Walking to class, we passed it each morning, the white metal fence next to the British War Cemetery, but I had never thought to venture in. Accustomed as I was to Australia's closed-door policy when it came to hospitals, I had perceived it as impenetrable.

---

[22]I walked in the desert and 'climbed' the mountain.

'Not here,' said Sam in a whisper. 'They've got me working in the ER. If you want, I'm sure I could get you in.'

'*B'Ivrit*!' chastised Margalit, overhearing us, and so Sam and I went back to talking about more mundane things, our secret written smugly across our faces.

I soon discovered, however, that to become a *mitnadevet*[23] at Hadassah was a mission in itself. The office was open during rather select hours and so, after a couple of failed attempts, I finally found myself in front of two stern ladies and a form written only in Hebrew.

They watched me struggle. Bored, perhaps by my lack of language, or the thought of *yet another girl who thinks she'll come to Israel for 'the experience' and then she'll cry home to Mum and Dad that nobody helped her*. I tried to read their frown. *Pah!* it said. *We came here with nothing, our desolate parents given no choice but to build this infant country.* Their home, our homeland, Israel's inception reinstating the diaspora, and between us a mutual, though well-meant, misunderstanding.

Security before bureaucracy, directness before warmth. Different priorities. A passport ominous in being required to send a parcel and yet the only thing necessary to gain a white coat and name tag for unquestioned access to the hospital.

As I was leaving, volunteer sheet in hand but ignorant to what I'd actually signed up for, one of the women stopped me.

---

[23]Volunteer (female).

'*Zot Yafa*,' that's pretty, she said pointing to my skirt, '*m'ai-foh*?' (From where?)

'*M'Sydney*' I replied, '*aifoh ani garah.*' (Where I live.)

'*B'emet*,' in truth, she smiled, '*yesh li sham mishpacha*,' (I have family there.)

And in that I understood. To be Jewish here was a laden truth, in many ways irrelevant. To be Aussie: well, that was a better start!

Chapter 4: *Cheshvan*

We woke in the desert surrounded by school children. With trained eyes, they'd spotted the electric sockets in the picnic hut and, never mind our sleeping bodies, were busy charging their phones. Tanya and I rolled over in our sleeping bags, Sandy sat up on the picnic table where she'd stationed herself, perhaps hoping her green beanie and look-to-kill might scare them away. But these kids had been born in the 21st Century. Liat, meanwhile, was sound asleep in the Bedouin tent further away. I respected that she knew herself; she'd joined us on this trip but was not quite ready to face the elements. The camp workers had flirted with her long into the night and she joined us for breakfast in great spirits. We gritted our teeth and smiled back. Perhaps our princess had been the wise one after all!

L'chazor: to return

Can one ever return? It was I who chose the desert for our second trip, in the week between *ulpan* and semester. I who wanted to see the yellow sand, to hear the silence, to taste the sweetness of water as the sun burnt down on my back. Sandy had agreed, to compare this landscape with what she'd seen in

Jordan, sixty kilometres to our east … then Tanya, then Liat. Four girls with backpacks, heading south.

Students spilled out from the village on Monday morning. On the tram, we crowded in, each group telling the others where we were going: to Greece, to Tel Aviv. We were thought brave. In peak hour, our bus inched towards the train station. We jumped off, running down the hill, bags through the scanner, tickets bought, 'Come on, come on'. On board, we dozed until the train reached the junction at the ancient city of Lod. Coffee on the platform, new train, onwards, deeper to Beersheba, *Be'er sheva*, that city of the wells.

But we couldn't linger. A bus, now, to our destination. We, seated, the soldiers who piled on filling every empty space. Climbing over them, we left the bus at our junction, the colour palette unchanged: khaki uniforms for a khaki landscape. Dust and narrow trees. On realising that our host had decided where we would be arriving, ignorant of the truth, we scampered across the highway to Kibbutz Sde Boker. Down the lane breezed a woman on a bicycle as we looked upon neat lawns and desert flower beds.

Martin Luther King Jr. dreamt that all men would be equal. David Ben-Gurion had a dream that such equity might come when the desert was a source of life. The old bible logic that through a miracle might miracles come. In his hut in Sde Boker, Ben-Gurion entertained nobility, dignitaries, those who held the strings of power. *Look,* he wished to show them, *I've done my part of the bargain, I've shown you that barren ground can be made to flower, that life can go on after despair.*

How, now, can you enrich the world?

Too often, that question was forgotten as the war kept raging, as the soldiers kept marching left, right, left, right. But you'll catch fragments in the wind, hear it in the chatter of the olive pickers. It's why the desert keeps calling me back.

Shown to the guesthouse, we found we had the place to ourselves. By afternoon, Tanya had developed a fever so we put her to bed, busying ourselves playing cards at the dining table, realising that we were adults now, dependent on each other. When evening came, we heated pita and baked potatoes in the toaster oven. I bumped the top element and burnt a hole in my finger – cursing my own stupidity. When I was fifteen, I suffered third degree burns above my knee. It was an experience that called me in to focus – the first whisper of that word, depression. When I was eighteen, and in the Negev for the first time, I learnt that I had just missed out on a place in Medicine. High up on the narrow, sandy paths, I contemplated mortality. Now, as the pain seared through me, I became determined. I would gain a grip on myself.

Morning broke and with it Tanya's fever. In the communal dining room, we were smiled upon by the *kibbutzniks*, who were simply dressed, the buffet breakfast part of their life's routine. Stewed fruits and fresh yoghurt nourished us; coffee for Liat, for whom a morning could not start without, and chocolate powder for Sandy, wanting in vices. Young men in the fields smiled at us as we made our way to Ben-Gurion's house, the physical life shining with a new allure.

As the others absorbed themselves in history, I drank in the house half-made of books. It had never occurred to me that I was 'like them', but suddenly I recognised my ancestors in the photographs, Eastern Europeans who had settled and toiled the land. Like David Grün, before he was Ben-Gurion, in Israel, or in South Africa like my family.[24] To find Polish culture in my blood, unexpectedly, years down the track – did my wondering start then?

By mid-morning we were back on the road. Hailing the bus, we found it as full as the day before, all khaki, bodies, rucksacks, Uzi guns. Soldiers invited us to sit on their laps, but we opted to perch on their packs. At a highway petrol station, we stopped for a break and I watched as Sandy surveyed the conscripts. Our age and yet transformed by discipline … It would be Sandy's destiny come next September. Did it frighten her?

Left, right, left, right, onwards to Mitzpe Ramon. *L'chazor*, to return. On my school-leavers' trip, we'd had a week of free choice: to stay in Jerusalem and learn politics, to join the army for a week in *Gadna*, or to hike the Ramon crater. To me there was no choice. We'd travelled into the *machtesh*,[25] spent our first night at an organised camp and then wandered further and further into the wilderness, erecting tents on flat ground.

I'd remembered the camp site and tried to arrange to stay

---

[24]My great-grandparents independently left Eastern Europe before WWII. They settled in South Africa where my grandparents and parents were born. As my parents left South Africa before I was born, however, joining my maternal family in Australia, I do not associate myself at all with the country. Yet it is too long since we have been in Europe to call myself European.
[25]Crater.

there. But when I rang the number, I was told it had closed. 'We have a tent in town now,' the man said in Hebrew. 'How about you stay there and I'll drive you down to the crater, for a fee.' Naturally. Unable to afford any of the posh hotels, I accepted but was perplexed. Why would the campsite close? Arriving in town, I spotted the restaurant the man had mentioned, but his tent was very well hidden! Adjacent was an information point and, on the premise of needing a map, I went to inquire.

Never have I been so laughed at. When the man serving me found how we'd been conned, he laughed so hard I thought we'd be punished for our gullibility. The campsite closed, no! It had been taken over by the park authorities. The man I'd spoken to was the old, fuming, owner who, eventually, was rung and thoroughly chastised. Equipped with a trail map and bus timetable, we headed back into the town. The trick had cost us. The bus we'd been on would have taken us right to the crater but now we'd have to wait. The thought of an hour and a half in the midday sun was too cruel to imagine.

When in Ramon, do as the Ramons do! At both sides of the junction stood adolescents trying to hitch a lift. From Mitzpe Ramon, there is only one road to Eilat; all traffic flows in the same direction. With four of us, we felt a safety in numbers but as cars flew past, we realised it would be difficult to find a lone driver.

Time ticked on until a shiny black car pulled over next to us. An elderly man sat in the front. The seats were covered in scraps of newspaper and an orange shirt hung in the window.

The fluent English of our driver was a welcome surprise. 'Where you girls going?' he enquired. We told him we were going to hike the crater. 'Not to Eilat?' he said with a wink. 'I own hotels there, I'll give you 60% off.' We laughed, thinking him a jokester.

'You know I built this road,' he said as we navigated the hair-pin bends. 'I'd drive faster, but I'd scare you.' We laughed again. 'You know,' he continued, 'people wonder why I drive. I'm a chairman of an airline, you see, I could fly for free.' What a character, we thought, but we agreed that, 'Yes,' the scenery was beautiful and, 'Yes,' we'd want to drive too. With great consideration, he dropped us at the bus stop, doing a U-turn to check that we were on the right path, and then as he drove off he offered to fetch us on Thursday morning. Had we known that everything he'd said was true, we might have taken his number.

***

The campsite lay five kilometres from the road. One behind the other we walked, keeping a steady pace. The heat pushed us on – to stop was to die – and we triumphed as we reached each 1000 metre post. Morale is strangely measured; is that why God told the Israelites how long they'd walk the desert? Four kilometres, five kilometres, round one last corner and we'd arrived. The picnic hut beckoned with a promise of shade and, flinging packs on ground, we gave in to its call.

We hiked in the afternoon, exploring old Nabatean ruins, returning with the sun setting behind us, a coolness, now, to the air. Time ticked by, slowly. In a world of nothingness and end-lessness, one would be wise to discard one's watch. Let the sun shape the day; let appetite, or so we learnt as we devoured tinned tuna and indulged in ice-creams from the kiosk. Glee.

To sleep on the ground. To recognise your spine, your feet, the space you take up on this earth. Only for a bus to pull up with noisy children, but you try not to let them bother you, even when their shrieks pierce the air, even when you wake with them standing over you. Because you are here by your own volition. Not sent on a camp, not recommended by a parent or friend. Here, simply, because you wanted to be.

And so we hiked all that day. Four women, utterly alone in the world, except for when we were stopped by a ranger who wondered if we wanted a lift ... and we said, no. I had a com-fort, then, in my body. A confidence, too. To walk was to be free and it pains me that illness stole that liberty. Health can be regained but a shattered confidence takes much more to repair. I've seen it in Sandy, whose time in the army dimmed her wanderlust spirit. Today, I look under layers to find the girl who lay with me in the shade, up on the rocks at the side of the *wadi*. [26] When we were there it was a dry ravine; in winter it would be a flowing stream. Waters that nurture versus waters that take. Liat grew in that desert. Israel enriched her. She bloomed, and so she stayed. I tried to go back, but failed. Now I know that life will tell me when it's time.

We left the desert in the morning's first light. Back down the sand path, one kilometre, two kilometres, towards the road. In

---

[26] Arabic: valley.

the still-cool air, we made good time and so stopped halfway to watch the sun grace the skies. If that was east, then we were heading south. Did we think of it? Or were we led by our onward destination, life bound by foregone conclusions, until they cease? But is ingenuity not borne from what does not go to plan, do stories not lie in the gaps of expectation?

Our bus, you see, did not arrive.

In today's age, we expect our phones to solve our problems. If a bus is late, then better than prophecy, they should declare when it is to come. But at that time Israel was still in the paper age and so when we rang the bus company, desperate for a firm answer, we were instead told:

'We will know the bus is late when it does not arrive in the town.'

And we would know how late we were when we missed our connection.

Late. No bus.

Later. Tour buses drove past us, empty, headed for the town. We stuck our hands out, hoping one might offer us a lift. But no one did.

Later still. Bus after bus went by, 56 empty seats but no room for us.

Almost, but not yet, dangerously late. A bus pulled up.

Through the open window, the driver asked us our destination. Mitzpe Ramon, we told him. He gestured to the passenger door in reply. It was only then that we realised that the bus front was a literal façade. Attached through some feat of engineering was a truck body, all bench seats and stripped back floors. We climbed up, suddenly scared, until Sandy spotted an (Israel Defence Forces) IDF flag on the rear wall. It is the only time I have ever found the symbol comforting.

Our driver was a patriot, the truck an army transport vehicle. Official, or not, we couldn't be sure. Shell casings littered the floor and Sandy, on sighting them, broke into laughter. 'Typical,' she said, 'for me to end up on an army truck'.

In silence, our driver navigated the hairpin bends. The engine roared as we got higher, closer to the town. And then we were there, the door opening to signal our arrival, we shouting our thanks as our saviour pulled away. 15 minutes. Just enough time to buy coffee and bagels for lunch!

On the bus to Dimona we laughed at how our parents would never have let us leave the house if they'd known what we'd get up to. A few years later some boys hitchhiking in the settlements were murdered and my deeds took on a new solemnity.

But then, our greatest concern was when the bus we tried to board was full, and with soldiers' laps this time denied, we thought we would be stranded. But it turned out there was a bus run by a private company so we ran and caught it and travelled to Dimona in comfort, only to arrive and our promised driver not be there. Soon a car pulled up and the man told us he was our ride and so we got in … scared, sure, aware of what could happen, of course … But we did there what we would never do at home.

Why?

Perhaps because we trust more in a land of freedoms. Is bureaucracy not the enemy of faith? On our day in the crater, our midday rest had been disturbed by a bunch of religious schoolgirls. For what Israeli's call a *tiyul*, a trip, we call a hike. Life there is, or at least was, unpolished but in many ways that's what made it more vibrant.

And so we found ourselves on a camel ranch in the middle of the desert. Our hosts greeted us warmly and then showed us to our beige hut: 'hideous' in Western parlance, 'nature little disturbed' in mine. In the afternoon we slept under a tree, interrupted only by the owners' dog and then as we waited for evening, and our camel ride, we returned to our room and seated on the floor, stripped off our shirts and devoured chocolate in our sports-bras.

The desert was changing us.

Time disappears as you ride a camel along the ancient 'Incense Route'. In Finland, I'd walked along another trade route, marvelling at humanity's mastering of the world. From freezing forests, to scorching deserts, harnessing hoofed animals to walk, and cross borders for trade, a language more powerful than any tongue.

On our trek, we communicated with our guide in Hebrew. Until Sandy wished to ask something that exceeded her vocabulary and so switched to Arabic. Our guide, Jamil, almost fell off his camel. But his respect for us grew.

Our camels walked on, unhurried, their bodies swaying like dancers as we sat with an unrivalled view. Jamil turned them from transport to creatures as he told us about their habits and personal ways. Back at the ranch, he whispered for them to kneel, so we slid off, thanking our new friends.

We showered, and wearing our cleanest clothes walked to the main hut for dinner. Kneeling on the mat, our right hands were washed and then we were served not as patrons but as guests. With our clean hand we ate and then we washed it again, to drink sweet desert tea.

Then with the sky now dark, the camels retired and our hosts smoking on the veranda, we returned to our hut. Closing the flap window, we settled onto our mats and slept deeply.

***

The name of my camel was Aliyah ...

It was while I was in Israel that my Dad assented for me to formally change my name from Nicole to Nicky (the informal change having been made when I was but a few days old). When I'd first asked him, I'd not understood his reticence. To say 'but Nicole is the name we gave you' seemed, to me, absurd when to call me Nicky had likewise been my parents' decision. But though I fought it and though, as Hodel tells Tevye,[27] I was seeking his approval, not his permission, I found that I could not go against his wishes.

Tradition!

In later life I learnt that to be like Hodel and date a Perchik was permissible, but to be like Chava was, well … But as awful as they were, those arguments with Dad helped me to arrive at a new clarity. He had, through immigration, fallen not only into the role of being our breadwinner but also our patriarch, a bastion of *Yiddishkeit*,[28]. And though I had always appreciated, and shared in, his facilitation of ritual practice, I had overlooked his spirituality.

Some might call it superstition but a name, in Judaism, is a covenant changed only in circumstances of life-threatening illness. So, what to me was an issue of identity – exacerbated by having a last name which is difficult-to-pronounce – was to Dad, a matter of breaking a bond. And his perception might have remained unchanged if not for a conversation he had with one of his Korean patients who, finding that her birth-name meant something else entirely in English, had bestowed upon herself the new name, Gloria, in praise of God.

By this time, I had patients of my own … From Muhamed to Mariam, Youssef to Yitzchak, all of God's prophets walked through, or were delivered, to my door. My job at Hadassah was as a *mitnadevet E.K.G*, an ECG volunteer, working in the

[27]The Dairyman', protagonist of *The Fiddler on the Roof.*
[28]Yiddish: literally, Jewishness.

Emergency Room. Whoever they prayed to, they hoped not to see me again.

It is hard for me to write about Hadassah, in part because I have written about it before. In many ways it was that story about how the hospital was an island of peace in a world of conflict, a place where Jews and Arabs not only worked side by side, but were treated side by side, that motivated me to write this book. And yet, because of that, I fear doing Hadassah a disservice, that it deserves a whole book, not a few pages, and that by writing about it I will oversimplify its worth. Or that I will not be believed, for what goes on at Hadassah, especially where I was, in Mount Scopus, on the border of East and West Jerusalem, is so at odds with the world's perception of Israel that anything I say will sound ludicrous. But let that word, instead, be miraculous.

My first shift was on a Tuesday afternoon. There is an adage in medicine that to learn a procedure you have to 'watch one, do one, teach one' and, following this model, Sam was left to 'show me the ropes'. Unfortunately, whilst he was an excellent teacher, he hadn't quite mastered the second step and thus our ECG's came out with lines all over them as if a child had been let loose with a pen.

Fortunately, however, most of our cases were not life threatening. So many things can lead to a patient presenting with chest-pain and thus our job was to rule out the more serious ailments. There were the patients who would have been shocked had we found anything, the public health system being a good way to get out of a less favourable afternoon (there was always at least one soldier in the bay) and then there were the true emergency cases at which time I was pushed out of the way, the curtain drawn and my ears the only thing I had to discern what was going on.

At first, I was paged as 'E.K.G.' and it was as a nurse was trying to learn my name that she asked if it was my uncle who also worked there. No, I said, to an uncle, though I did have some (distant) Gluch relatives in Israel, so a relation wasn't impossible. But a Paul? No. Told that he'd be working that afternoon, I became intrigued to meet this nominal twin – except that it turned out the nurse had made the same mistake as so many others, presuming my name, like the composer's, to be Gluck.

Pol's (or Paul's) Hebrew fluency belied his Commonwealth past and so it was only when we started talking that I learnt he was from Melbourne. Finding out I was from Sydney, he asked if I knew his brother, and I, gobsmacked, said that not only did I know him, but that Ben often led services at my *shul*. More than that, his two other brothers (one deceased) had been teachers at my father's school in South Africa.

From generation to generation, over three continents … the world suddenly seemed rather small. Dad delighted in the story. Having always believed he knew all the Gluck sons, he'd been disappointed to learn there was one living in Israel. That I had closed the circle, by such chance, was to him a symbol of a guiding fate. The true miracle of this meeting is that I never saw Paul again. He suggested I work with him on Sunday afternoons, a man and woman needing to be present at all times, but when Sunday came, my boss rang asking where I was. She needed me in the mornings, and asked me to come, with haste. So 9 am - 2 pm became my slot. I never saw Paul's fellow worker from that first afternoon, an Englishwoman, again either. Yet our one conversation later led me to stay in a convent in Ein Karem … but that's another story.

Gluch, Gluck, Nicole, Nicky… what's in a name? So much in Israel (where my choice to use that term, and not Palestine already marks me) where one's religious affiliation, even more, religiosity can be so easily inferred from what is a combination of letters that define us, and yet exists nowhere. Where is our name, should be the question? On our heart, our soul? And why can't we have concomitant identities? In the Bible, characters are known as many things, Hadassah, for example, being another name for Queen Esther, and with transliteration, things morph (as T.E. Lawrence told his editor, in no uncertain terms).

Indeed the reason I met Paul, and the Englishwoman, and worked from then on with Larry, a Canadian, is because the ECG machines required English proficiency. And so our patients would arrive, with their Arabic names, which would be transliterated into Hebrew upon admission, which I'd then unwittingly mispronounce (Hebrew has no vowels), and be corrected, to determine what should be written in Latin script. And all the meanwhile they'd tease me that Nicky wasn't a girls' name, at least not where they were from, whilst those who could read Hebrew would see that my badge said Nicole and ask if I was French. And then there were the religious Jewish patients who demanded to know my Hebrew name:

'Naomi? An important woman. You are in Israel now; that is who you should be.'

And I'd smile while I used cotton wool to wipe their wrists and ankles, placed the clamps, wiped their chest – sorry it's cold! – lay the blue device against their sternum. And while I told them to lie still – no wriggling, no eating, no talking on the phone – my own heart would pound as I stood by the machine and hoped for normal lines:

… P.QRS.T …

Whatever your name, whatever the alphabet, it only takes five letters to know if you're alive.

Chapter 5: November

Five years. What is it in the life of a 25-year-old? Everything? Nothing? In October 2013, I started university in Jerusalem. Five years later I'm sitting here, writing about it, in London with everything as new, as different as it was then but so much less overwhelming. For it is not the first time.

Back then. Heart racing, hands sweating as you stand there, on the outskirts of the campus, utterly lost. Monday morning, the second day of term. People smile, greet each other, walk past, on and on in a well-rehearsed routine. While you, you feel you've ventured far enough ... finding the bus, getting yourself from Mount Scopus across the city to Givat Ram.

Givat Ram. This campus, where you stood a year before. But it was summer then, the place yours to inhabit. More, you were dignitaries. Student volunteers guided you and the 350 other young, chosen, scientists. You were the gratified; now you are a child.

'Excuse me?' 'Can you help me?' you implore, as you search for a building no one has heard of. '*B'vakashah*,' please, 'I'm looking for the Edmund and Lily Safra Center for Brain Sciences.'

'*Mah?*' What?

'The Centre for Brain Sciences.'

'Brraiin Scionsez ... ah, *Midei Ha'Moach*, yes?'

'Yes.' You blush. You had not thought to wonder what it would be in Hebrew. And as your presumptions are cut down, you fall from your loft. The clever little girl from Australia come to learn science with the grown-ups. You're not special here, a land of wunderkinds, of toughened soldiers. Work out who you are or go home.

The Brain Center, or ELSC as we called it, turned out to be on the far reaches of the campus. The part where earth was being turned for the first time. From the correct bus stop, one scrambled up a dirt path, onto the cement, through the glass door at the back of the Life Sciences building, and up the stairs to the top floor.

The world has since caught up with Israel's 'start-up nation', where the dream is a couch, a coffee machine and a whole lot of innovation, but then, having seen very little beyond a classroom, I was stunned. Befitting the heights, ELSC was less a student building than a penthouse.

Students sat on the couches, coffee (in ELSC glasses) in hand. A corridor separated the staff offices from the classrooms, modular more than anything, one large one small. The secretary rushed around, kissing familiar faces and greeting new ones. I, however, was promptly told not to expect a coffee cup. 'You are not one of ours,' Esti said.

That rankled me, slightly, never having been one for clubs. And as much as the set-up impressed me, I felt a twinge at the loss of Israeli simplicity. Months later, though, while sitting on those same couches, I watched the staff (each brighter than the next) turn plans for their new building this way and that, arguing, nay, insisting, in a way that only Israelis can.

If you're going to put lipstick on a pig, you'd better buy a dress to match.

As a child, to say that Maths was my favourite subject was to extol some dreadful secret. Fortunately, however, by the time I learnt this I had been nurtured by such brilliant *female* mathematicians that I was prepared to live with the shame. To me, numbers were more than a world of order and logic. They spoke, and in their conversations the world felt calm and right.

Of the many things that appealed, I was drawn to the universality of Maths. That said, I had not given thought to dialectic differences – that x is not 'eks' the world over. That first Monday morning I became acquainted with 'iks', a relic of the German background of Israel's first professors. Where, too, in Australian abbreviating fashion we have *cos* and *sin* and *tan*, in Jerusalem the functions took their full names.

'Seen iks over co-seen iks ekwals?'

'*Tangent iks.*'

'*Nachon.*' Correct.

Our teacher, Dalya, was sweet and young. A PhD student, she was at the end of the five-year journey my classmates had just begun. ELSC is a centre for computational neuroscience. It's proudly interdisciplinary, drawing the most talented, rather than the most specialised students, from Israel and abroad. The first two years were therefore about laying the ground-work, content before application, but there was no acclimation period. The hard work began on day one. Fail a course (a concept interpretable by the staff) and you could repeat it; fail again, and you were kicked out.

The tension, thus, was always palpable. Perhaps that's why I was denied a coffee cup; I was a free agent, in the enviable position where I was exposed to everything, but nothing I did mattered. I could enjoy the challenge, be it in Dalya's calculus class, my twice-weekly physiology lectures or the delightful world of linear algebra I entered each Wednesday morning.

The only professor who did not forgive my freedom was, ironically, an Australian. Perhaps he thought I was giving the country a bad name. Or perhaps it was the nature of his course. I was there to learn cognitive processes, but all I felt was scrutinised.

Whatever I did, I could not help standing out. Though the course was international by design, the students were pre-dominantly Israeli. That being so, they were also older than

Masters students back home. Take the two-three year compulsory army service and add to that one or two gap years, a completed Bachelors and time for contemplation, and many of my classmates were nearing 30.

They weren't about to take a 19-year-old under their wing.

I had no choice, then, but to become friends with Nell, aged twenty, Dutch and with dyed hair. I initially thought her like me only in our difference. But as the weeks went on, I found we had much in common, the information elicited not through conversation, but Nell's necklaces.

'Ah,' noticing her scorpion pendant, 'so you're a Scorpio too?'

'Yes,' she smiled. 'When's your birthday?'

'November 10.'

'No way! Mine too.'

On our next meeting, she wore a flute charm.

'You're a flautist!'

'Yes, actually I studied at the Conservatoire in Amsterdam before my Bachelor's.'

'Really, that was always my dream, but in Paris …'

Another day she wore an N necklace. But we already knew

we had that in common.

And so it became our ritual, Nell and I, to work together, she helping me turn numbers into computer code, I clarifying some of the concepts.

We talked while we worked and one day I told her about Gerard, a Dutch man I'd helped to find his Australian family.

'I used to work at the Jewish Museum …'

'No shit!' Nell interjected in her standard fashion, while always looking to check no one had heard. 'I used to work in the Museum in Amsterdam. In the children's department…'

Those are bonds you cannot invent. They're uncanny, and Israel makes it a habit to expose them.

***

Back at Mount Scopus …

How had I forgotten that our philosophy classes began with a discussion of 'Babel'?

On Tuesday afternoons our lecturer, my advisor, Jack would pace around his classroom, expectant …

I sit here, writing a book to be titled, *The Universal Language*, remembering so much of what came after 'Babel' and believing that it is the 'after' which influenced where I am today.

I've been musing, as I do almost perpetually, on language and conversation and why some of us can speak without words. Yet the fact that our philosophy class sat on the hills of Mt Scopus discussing that fateful tower had slipped into some recess of my mind from where, in guilt, I must now retrieve it.

Let's speak in three languages just for a moment – *Migdal Ha'Bavel, La Tour de Babel,* The Tower of Babel – and think about the origins of translation.

Back in Sydney after my study period in Israel, I found myself missing the Hebrew language. I ventured up to the seventh floor of my university library and, expecting purely academic texts, discovered that Amos Oz had once made it onto the syllabus.[29] His hardback books, jackets removed, were like a deliverance: the characters' flaws in keeping with my own, the same brown bread comforting, the same love of nature and political confusion writ onto the page. Such is his divisiveness that for a reader to like Oz, I have since learnt from his dissenters, is to be clichéd or, from his supporters, to find immediate friends. I shy away from both sides. My encounter with Oz was chance, his books, deeply personal to me. When I need them, they are a great comfort. At other times, I cast them aside, the words slipping under my skin and taking hold of my greatest insecurities. Once, I took his books to my biochemistry labs, for entertainment while the chemicals we obediently pipetted did what they did, with the same lack of understanding as we had about their function. My classmates sat on their phones and so I read, and at one point I remarked on an oversight in the translation and they looked

---

[29]Amos Oz, *To Know a Woman*, London: Vintage, 1992.

at me, dumbfounded. I realised that to them, Babel had never fallen. Words were simply 'in other languages'. But it is in translation, as George Steiner points out, that understanding occurs. (Steiner, with whom those philosophy classes began, before ... though his book was called 'After'.) *After Babel* – what rises from the chaos? The beauty of understanding, the pain of mis-understanding, or the destruction of not understanding. Our supplanting of English onto everything is not convenience, but denial.

To Steiner, Babel babbles as he contemplates *language* in its infancy, and our own.[30] For when does language start to shape us? When our tongue begins to form sounds, or before? As we sit in the babbling womb, or before? Is language coded into the four letters of our DNA?

To me, Babel is one step from bible. Some Jews believe that darkness descended upon the earth for three days when the Torah was first translated. Why? Not because we fear the vernacular. We are instructed to learn the language of any place we live. No, perhaps because it permits the thinking that: *'Bereishit barah Elokim et ha'shamaim v'et ha'aretz' is 'Au commencement, Dieu créa le ciel et la terre'* is 'In the beginning God created the heaven and the earth'. But they are not the same, and it is impossible to talk about religion until we accept that. And yet we do, every day.

Jack would walk as he talked. His kippah askew, he perched on tables, window ledges, expounding ideas and pointedly asking questions to which he did not want the answer. You'd

---

[30]George Steiner, *After Babel,* London: Oxford University Press, 1975.

try to speak, sweating as all eyes turned to you, until you learnt that nothing was ever correct, nor wrong, and from shuddering, you'd learn to sit in awe. The third stage was feeling permitted to question.

Jack did not encourage fraternisation. His classes were without interval – one-act plays that demanded your full attention. After an hour and a half, the curtain would go down and we'd spill out (the actor did not like to discuss his performance), sometimes talking with all our bottled energy, other times preferring contemplative silence.

One afternoon, I walked home with a French-Canadian classmate. Classical music and cups of tea … From her window we watched the sun set over the Dome of the Rock. Kisses, 'we should do this again,' – then I went back to my apartment. But we never did it again, the singularity of Jack's lessons almost forbidding repetition.

In the second week, Leanora joined the class. At first, a jealousy raged; Jack was mine! But slowly this claim revealed a deeper truth; I was afraid to let others see that which affected me. In my youth, I had been a brain, my heart buried beneath others' expectations. Leanora, open, emotive, gave me no space for privacy. And so our souls became entwined with a platonicity that made it pure, the warmth still easily conjured after all these years.

In our apartment, on the low blue couch, we'd discuss the readings, and Leanora would tell me of Rilke and Foucault and love, always love. It was only later that I had ideas to share … and when I did, she listened. Leanora worked in common spaces, I in my room, pages everywhere. Sandy's gift Bible sat on my bed as I searched its English pages to make sense of Steiner, who was born French.

And by this time, we'd moved on to Jacques Derrida who writes so wisely of the Hebrew God, "He *at the same time* imposes and forbids translation."[31] But this was still 'before'. Before what happened which led me to sit, today, writing a thesis on simultaneity … before what made me contemplate why it matters that *'Bereishit barah'* is not *'Au commencement'* is not 'In the beginning'. Because when I studied *Babel*, I was a scientist, I was to be a doctor. I was working in Hadassah Hospital, finding that I could speak without words. That being kissed by an Arabic grandma after you've put on her socks needs no translation and that death has its own particular sound.

After, I ended up in London; I went to Morocco; I read Elias Canetti. And sitting in Hampstead, where Canetti himself used to live, I read these words:

'What is there in language? What does it conceal? What does it rob one of? … in Morocco I made no attempt to acquire either Arabic or any of the other Berber languages. I wanted to lose none of the force of those foreign sounding cries.'[32]

The beauty of the chaos, a search for understanding. It all be-

---

[31]Jacques Derrida, 'Des Tours de Babel', trans. Joseph F. Graham, *Difference in Translation*, Ithaca: Cornell University Press, 1985.
[32]Elias Canetti, *The Voices of Marrakech*, trans. J.A. Underwood, London: Penguin, 2012.

gan with 'Babel', the knowledge that language is a part of us: *la langue*, the tongue. Let us not be the ones to cut it out.

***

But the heart has a language of its own ...

I should have told her (Mum), that I bumped into him at the bus stop. But it was a Thursday, I was rushing between classes, and perhaps nothing would come of it.

'Nicky?'

I'm lost in thought, my attention fixed on the bus's approach, startled: 'Oh, hello ...'

'So you are in Jerusalem now?' The physicist's quantum observation.

'Yes, I've been here a few months, studying at ELSC,' I said, while deducing he was not in contact with the other Israelis I knew. 'And you, Misha, where are you headed?'

'I live down there,' he said, pointing to the campus dorms, always there, but never noticed before. My bus pulled up.

'Should I come with you?'

Why not, if he had nowhere else to be? I got on, greeted the driver, took my right-hand window seat. He, merely joking, walked off.

Relieved, I removed Derrida from my bag, checked the Steiner essay was still in place. It was a Thursday, the end of the week. I'd had physiology, was off to philosophy, before heading back to ELSC for the weekly seminar. It was November, not yet cold. That night I would meet Sandy and Tanya in the city, and attempt, but fail, to find them clothes. From the shops to the Old City via Jaffa Gate. Find Leonora and explore a mediaeval fair. I told Mum all of this, but not that I saw Misha. It was a moment. And I was shy.

I should have told her (Nell) that he suggested we meet for coffee. But considering that after the camp he wrote to me but once, I did not anticipate our date with any feeling greater than curiosity.

The year before, I'd found him alluring, chastising myself for liking the man who didn't look Jewish, but thinking it was because he was also the eldest at university whereas the others were still at school, and because it was he who suggested we – as a group – go dancing. But we didn't, we just played cards until the early hours. He sat on the bus with Kate and me each morning, and I never knew if he was looking at me or her with her vibrant hair.

And I was shy. For upon realising Wednesday was the only possible day, I told Nell that we could not work together as I had an appointment. Which I did, but not at 2 pm.

I should have told her (Sandy) how much I wanted a boyfriend. But you're not meant to say what you wished for, especially blowing out candles on the cake someone's made specially for you. It was Friday, two days before my birthday. That morning I'd received my exam timetable; more than three weeks between my first exam and the last, the idea of a family holiday now in ruins. The tears would fall, tomorrow, but that day I'd considered options, made plans, between going to the mall, making dinner, attending *shul* and coming home to friends who'd used the kitchen in my absence. Beaming.

I felt so touched. Could not think of the last time friends had remembered, considered, done something for me. And it continued, for on Sunday I woke to balloons and then went to Hadassah, where no one knew. So the day was never tarnished. After so many years of people forgetting, so many years of waiting, hoping, that the phone would ring … on my 20th birthday I instead took pleasure when my name was paged, on doing ECG's, inputting names, date of births, guarding, secretly my own.

In the evening, we caught the tram. To the stop before the *Shuk*. And down in some secret place, we ate *injera*[33] with the locals. Our hands washed, as per Ethiopian custom, the bread forming both plate and cutlery, we scooped the food into our mouths while the TV played African pop. And after we'd washed our hands once more, we posed for a photo, our stranger turned photographer suddenly an artiste, insistent on the perfect shot. So we're captured in good humour, a laugh in our eyes, the photo all light and red-eye, unframeable. Perfect, as I am shy.

I should have told her (Tali, my sister) about the arrangement,

[33]Ethiopian flatbread.

for she always hoped that I would share. But after it, I did not go home, but rather went to settle the room where I would stay in January (for six weeks now, not four) and when I woke the next morning, it was the day of her formal back in Australia and her date had taken ill. Mum was distraught. And I was distraught. And Tali, as always … well I wished I knew. So I sent her my support, and my sympathy, and was glad when her friend consented to join. And in spite of everything, she looked majestic, in a purple robe from Perth, with earrings from Jerusalem, her flowing hair from God.

I should have told her, I should have known how. But when she came to Jerusalem, we spoke of other things … and it was cold, and we were hungry, and I was shy.

I should have told her (Leonora) that I was scared of chivalry. That when Misha and I met at Belgium House, a haven of sun and sculpture hidden on campus, I tried to buy my own coffee. But he worked there so said I could have it for free, the cake too. I might have told her how in place of conversation, a 'catch-up' of the past year, he instead told me of his family. How he was eight when he'd come from Belarus to Israel, how he had a younger brother, had grown up in Arad …

I might have told her, if I hadn't woken to find her standing in my room, at two in the morning, heart-broken, distressed, at learning her girlfriend had moved on. So instead I comforted her, and in the ensuing days tried not to speak of love. And I was shy.

If only I had told any of them what he said to me on parting:

'Perhaps we should do this again.' I might have told them, had he called. But instead it was chance that brought us together and being so fond of coincidence, I took the good from that, not the truth.

If only I had not kept him secret, for it added a dangerous allure.

Chapter 6: *Kislev*

A Rabbi I know, a young man, recently moved houses in London. Sitting in his freshly painted living room, he told of the mover's surprise at what he'd found in so many of the boxes … books.

'You see,' the Rav tried to explain, 'I'm a Rabbi, so what's in those boxes is the very essence of what I do …'

'Sure,' said the mover. 'I get it, but you Jews are meant to be clever. Aren't these on Kindle by now?'

Paper, pages, the smell. The tables laid out, for books, the ladders, for books. To enter a library is for me to enter a world of delight.

The history that lines every wall, not for what lies between the covers but for who held them. Illicit margin notes and coffee stains, tickets left marking pages. To me it enthrals.

To enter, thus, the mathematics library at Givat Ram, in the Einstein building, his bequeathed papers lying just over the road, was to combine two pleasures:

Words, so artfully put to describe that more exact, and yet at times more abstract, handling of numbers.

The wisdom of linear algebra in a volume small enough to fit in my pocket. Tomes by the names in my textbooks … it was like I'd been let in on a secret, and I looked around lest someone find me undeserving of the privilege.

***

De-r-ri-da,

I hear it now like the opening of Beethoven 5, not ominous so much as a proclamation:

De-r-ri-da.

Fate: It was one of the few times in my life I was sure of something. That I was seeing something self-evident, that others had simply missed. Thus, not that there might be an analogy between matrices and Derrida's philosophy but that there *was* an analogy. It was only Jack who was the sceptic.

It didn't help that he didn't like maths.

No, that's not right.

It didn't help that he feared maths, that numbers were his, '*Mysterium tremendum*. A frightful mystery, a secret to make you tremble,'[34] as we have permitted them to be for so many

---

[34]Derrida, *Gift of Death*, p 54.

intelligent people … like the one who raised me.

I took his fear as inspiration. I would proselytise, enlightening as to the gift that is mathematics to resolve the conundrum that is the gift of death:

And God said [to Abraham], 'Please take your son, your only one, whom you love – Isaac – and go to the land of Moriah; bring him up there as an offering upon one of the mountains … '[35]

Was there a story, in Torah, I hated more than *Akedat-Yitzhak*?

The Binding of Isaac.

A conducting teacher once told my class that to be freed from the score, we should conduct as if the music were being written whilst we were on the podium. The composer handing up freshly-inked pages so that Beethoven's symphony is as revelatory today as it was in 1808. The Torah should be read in the same way. Sure the stories follow an annual cycle (with the Akedah tied to the week before my birthday) but whether Isaac will be unbound, should never seem guaranteed.

It is because of this (as the Torah says) that complex discussion of Jewish texts has gone on for millennia. Boys become men as they don black suits and, in pairs, seek for insight (not revelation) at *yeshiva*…[36] Orthodox women attend seminary,

---

[35]Genesis 22:2.
[36]Literally, sitting. An education institute that focuses on the study of religious texts.

those in Reform can now become Rabbis, and with their liberalism colour the teachings in ways their antecedents would never have imagined. But it is just a different legitimacy. So engrained is the notion that even Jews who do not believe in God cannot but help themselves... Erich Fromm, the great psychologist, was a Talmud scholar and Derrida ... well something made him seek out Emmanuel Levinas:

To contemplate how in a religion that forbids human sacrifice, Abraham can be told to offer up his son ...

Derrida knew that he did not know.

But he knew that it was important as the Rabbis chose for the *Akedah* to be read not once, but twice each year. Isaac's birth, for the first day of Rosh Hashanah, and his almost death for the second.

Romantic, almost, considering it's the Day of Judgement. But if it were so simple, why sustain the argument for so many years?

'Abraham's willingness is proof of his devotion,' say those who believe that this is God's greatest test.

'He knows God won't go through with it, that's why he can,' say those who think Abraham has the answer sheet.

No, I rallied against the first, not wanting Abraham to be a murderer. How absurd, I said to the second, not liking a God who plays games.

It's a paradox, said Derrida, and I believed him. But Jack wanted to know how? And more, why? Why must our great patriarch transgress ethics to affirm his faith? I told him that I might have (an) answer.

Answering it, as I was, for myself. Because I had always hated the story. Because when I'd come to Israel for the Asian Science Camp, I'd trembled at the sight of an Akedah sculpture outside the hotel. But any uncertainty I had about being there was soon quashed by the keynote speaker, Robert Aumann, who quoted Torah in a discussion of (mathematical) game theory and inspired me to leave Sydney and study in a place where scientists wore *kippot*. And at a time when I was uncertain about this decision, my lab partner happened to lend me Daniel Kahneman's 'Thinking, fast and slow'. And because of Kahneman, I learnt about the Center for the Study of Rationality, and because of that, I stopped fearing going to Israel, and in debt to that I attended the Sunday seminars where I understood little except that the speaker was interrupted by a man who thought he knew more about rationality. And that when he bored of this irrationality, Robert Aumann stood up. And like an oracle, spoke the only sense of the afternoon.

His words mixed with what I was learning, for my teacher taught matrices as if the components were characters. It was all so alive.

But none of this would have mattered had it not come to pass that on the day that Jack was to set the essay question, I met with him in his role of academic advisor. And finding that he could advise me very little as regarded ELSC (having never set foot on the campus), and not knowing how to advise me on his course, we turned instead to its content.

'The words are so similar,' I said to Jack, 'Derrida talks about the general, or ethical, realm and the singularity of faith, whereas matrices are termed regular and singular.'

I sketched one for him on a scrap of paper, a square where each box is filled by a number, like this:

$$A = \begin{array}{|c|c|} \hline 1 & 2 \\ \hline 3 & 4 \\ \hline \end{array}$$

and explained how what you searched for was the inverse of that matrix:

$$A^{-1} = \begin{array}{|c|c|} \hline a & b \\ \hline c & d \\ \hline \end{array}$$

its special complement, such that when you multiplied the two you got the identity matrix:

$$\begin{array}{|c|c|} \hline 1 & 2 \\ \hline 3 & 4 \\ \hline \end{array} \quad x \quad \begin{array}{|c|c|} \hline -2 & 1 \\ \hline 1.5 & -0.5 \\ \hline \end{array} \quad = \quad \begin{array}{|c|c|} \hline 1 & 0 \\ \hline 0 & 1 \\ \hline \end{array}$$

the same for each pair, every time, *bashert.*[37]

'But what has this got to do with Derrida?' Jack asked, 'and more importantly [and at this he became emphatic] why does Abraham *have* to be unethical?'

I told him that if he let me, I would show him (bravado) and perhaps he too so hoped I might resolve this unpleasant story,

---

[37]Yiddish: fate or destiny, used to refer to a person's soulmate.

as he gave me leverage to try. And then asked me why I had come to Israel.

He knew that I did not know, that one can only ever intimate at an answer ... or in Abraham's case, in Derrida's words, it's about knowing not to know.

De-r-ri-da, De-r-ri-da.

He who writes so complexly, whose sentences unfold like a stream of consciousness. I would try to simplify them through maths.

Why? Because numbers are discreet. Because I have always believed in them, because they are my comfort.

Because when Derrida talks about a dissymmetry, a gap in knowledge between God and Man I could say, but of course. For Aumann had told me how in game theory, everyone has a level of knowledge and that you can only know the levels below you. If you are level 6, you know all that exists at levels 1-5 but level 7, you can only guess at ... it's beyond your comprehension ... you have no idea what it is you do not know.

Rationality says that for equilibrium to be reached, two people must interact in a way that they can both intuit the actions of the other (the higher person lowering themself to the lower's plane). But this is not God's duty, and this is what Abraham understood, for faith is irrational. If God has infinite knowledge, Abraham could never know what lay between himself and divinity. Thus, when God asked him to sacrifice Isaac, he could only comply, and when Isaac asked him where the lamb was for the slaughter he could only say, 'God will provide.' If he had said, 'God told me to slaughter you,' he would have been putting God on his plane. Which would be denying faith. Abraham's leap was to accept this, to break from the right and wrong which man can determine, to transgress the ethical code.

Accepting, then, that man is finite. God is infinite, and singular. Monotheism in a nutshell.

But why was Isaac needed to prove this? Why is Abraham's greatest test whether he will give up his own son?

Because it proves that he cannot. That faith is contingent on continuity, it's the only thing that can get Man closer to infinity …

And so it is for all of Abraham's descendants. The father of nations, Judaism, Christianity and Islam each interpret the Akedah in a way that speaks to the religion's very essence.

Islam honours Ibrahim's willingness to sacrifice his son, a demonstration of his love for God over all others. That Allah provided a lamb is commemorated in the festival Eid al-Adha with families sacrificing livestock and sharing the meat with the poor.

Christianity contemplates whether Isaac might have been resurrected, and thus it is in this that Abraham has faith in God. As a lamb was instead provided, Jesus becomes the true *agnus dei* and before there was a New Testament, the Akedah was read on the day marking Jesus' birth.

Bless Sandy who said to me, 'We are just three faces of the same moon.'

If only we would see it.

So, to the mathematical perspective, that universal, unaligned:

Step 1: In the same way that all regular matrices have an inverse, and only ever have one solution, singular matrices break all the rules. Calling, 'for a betrayal of everything that manifests itself within the order of universal generality,'[38] singular matrices have no inverse. They have infinite solutions or none at all.

Step 2: In a regular matrix, each value is interdependent. It can be solved like any mathematical equation, eliminating one unknown at a time, until there is only one equation with one possible answer. This is not the case for singular matrices. Why? Because at least one of the values in a singular matrix has to be independent, defining the identity of a (dependent) other:

'And God said, 'Let us make Man in our image …''[39]

Without dependence, there is one solution. With dependence, paradoxically, comes infinite solutions.

---

[38]Derrida, *Gift of Death,* p 81.
[39]Genesis 1:26.

But not always.

When a singular matrix has only two dimensions, call it the interaction of two people, it is like parallel lines ... they never meet and thus the matrix is unsolvable.

To have one solution, two lines need only a point of intersection but to have infinite solutions they require a third line, a plane that traverses and takes them to infinity.

This plane, in the relation between God and Abraham, is Isaac. Between each pair, God and Abraham, Abraham and Isaac, Isaac and God can exist a viable relationship, but it is only when the three are co-existent that infinity, the singularity of faith is realised. Thus it is not only that Abraham cannot sacrifice Isaac, he would have undone everything by doing so.

De-r-ri-da,

De-r-ri-da.

Echoing: faith, fate, a hope for peace. Do we hear the call?

***

Of all the festivals in the Jewish calendar, Chanukah is the only one that originated in Israel. The festival of Purim recounts Jewish life in Shushan (today's Iran), while the biblical festivals, the ones on which we refrain from work, began in the desert. Yet, it could be asked whether Chanukah would have 'taken off' if not for the diaspora. As Jews found themselves in the cold reaches of the earth, and as their Christian neighbours celebrated Yuletide with food and song, why not but embrace the 'festival of light'? When, as the Yiddish poet pointed out, in a calendar filled with solemnity, it's a rare chance for joy:

Chanukah oy Chanukah	Chanukah, oh Chanukah
A yontif a sheyner,	A beautiful celebration.
A lustiker a freylekher	Such a cheerful and happy one,
Nisht do nokh azoyner	There is none like it.

There is none like it ... a festival unique for Ashkenazi Jews and for having found a place in the public consciousness. From the joy to the songs, the oily food and rather minor religious requirements, Chanukah is at once accessible and well placed for the Christian world, given a nod to, during what we term the 'festive season' and embraced by Chabad who can erect a public *Chanukiah*[40] to complement each same Christmas tree. Indeed, it is the archetypal chanukiah, metal with U-shaped branches often centred around a *Magen David*, which in many films is used to denote a character as Jewish. It's there on the mantlepiece, or falling out a suitcase as people flee in the War ...

For all of this, however, my personal relationship with the festival can at best be termed tangential. More so, ironic. It figures little in my childhood memories, partly because grow-

---

[40]Nine branch candelabra.

ing up in the southern hemisphere, where December days are long, candle lighting was something for after dinner, a pause in the evening or, when we were very little, just before bed. Then there was my Dad's reluctance about the commercial aspect, seeing the gift giving as purely an American sympathy, an apology to Jewish children for the lack of Christmas, and the fact we didn't have cousins to gather with and ... who knows?

At middle school in Sydney, it became my job to provide the instrumental accompaniment at the annual assembly. Not liking jam, the promised donut (*sufganiyah*) seemed anything but a reward! But it was more than teenage reticence which made me shy away from this particular public acknowledgement of my Jewish faith. Yes, Chanukah celebrates the miracle of the oil – that what remained of the sanctified liquid was enough to burn for one day but lasted, instead, for eight – but the miracle was only necessary because of the profanation of war. And I was born a pacifist.

'What brought you to Israel?' Jack had asked me and because I'd been waxing lyrical about my experiences, it was closely followed by, 'So why don't you stay?'

It was easy to stall, to blame family, language, opportunity... but it was also futile. Every Zionist has left family behind, whilst simultaneously hoping that their parents, for want of grandchildren, might follow. To acquire Hebrew, there was *ulpan* and opportunity... well yes, wages were low, housing exorbitant and traffic notorious but there was always a way. Had one the will— which I did not. But those words were hard to form. And equally futile.

'But you're here?'

'Yes.'

'And you're happy?'

'Yes.'

'And you admit that it hasn't always been easy to be Jewish in Australia?'

'Yes, but …'

It was as sure a lost argument as trying to convince an Australian that going to study in Israel did not make me a Zionist. Or, to a simpler point, that being Jewish did not make me Israeli:

I'm thinking of a conversation in a town in country NSW…

'Nice of you to come visit our Jane.'

'Well, she comes to Sydney so often, and anyway, I like to see the countryside.'

Jane's father nods, searching for something to say. 'So any plans for Christmas?'

'Not really… my family's Jewish so we just enjoy the day off.'

'Jewish, hmm. So were you born here or in Israel?'

'Here, but my parents aren't Israeli ...'

'No? I thought all Jews were from there.'

3000 years ago, I want to say. Before Jerusalem fell to the Romans, and before them, the Seleucids (Greeks) and before the first exile by the Babylonians with people herded like cattle as men fought for dominion and ...

'I won't live in a military state,' I told Jack, because some things never change.

Maoz tzur y'shuati l'cha na'eh l'shabe'ach.
O mighty stronghold of my salvation, to praise You is a delight.

How much easier it was to sing when I didn't understand the words, me, who shuns the Armistice poppy, who puts the Anzac rosemary in my pocket, not upon my lapel because I prefer to be numb than to contemplate war. How could I delight in the Maccabees' triumph? In how a priest became a warrior and how his son, the great Yehuda, hammered home a Jewish victory?

This festival which became motif, of struggle and conquest, for diaspora Jews, celebrating 'the great miracle that happened, there' until the day they spun their dreidel and it landed not on 'there' but 'here'. For Israel was the phoenix from the ashes for those who see it so, the restoration of Jerusalem to its people just as, centuries earlier, the Temple had itself been restored. Chanukah, oh Chanukah, it meant nothing to me … until I first went to Israel.

We sat beneath the stars. It was early, but the sun had long since set, and in the cooling air we pressed our bodies together, sharing our warmth. Our tents sat further, yonder, disappearing into the blackness of the surroundings. No light, no sound, no knowledge of where we were other than 'the Negev'. Sitting, now, resting our tired limbs for we had walked to this nowhere point. Awake with the dawn, on the road before sunrise, our bodies warming with the day climbing paths and then descending again, from there to here. And now that it was night, in the middle of December, or the dying days of Kislev, our guide took out a silver tray, placed candles in it and struck a match. And with a mellifluous voice he recited the prayer, and in the way he said the words, I believed him.

I was eighteen before I enjoyed Chanukah, before I understood that any pleasure I took from the festival could only be vicarious. On that first trip, I was provided with one view, that of my non-religious but deeply spiritual (and beautiful) guide. When I lived there, a year when the festival began in November, I saw it through a different lens every night.

On the eighth, through the eyes of Zionistic Americans. I taught them how to make *latkes*[41] and marvelled at how easily they were able to wave two flags.

---

[41]Yiddish, referring to the potato pancake eaten on Chanukah.

On the seventh night, I went to a concert with Leanora. On the sixth, my path crossed with Misha. He poured me wine at a housewarming party and the candles flickered like the twinkle in his eye.

On the fifth night, I saw the joy Chanukah brought the sick. On the fourth, we belatedly celebrated Thanksgiving.

On the third night, I was amongst Israelis, friends from the Asian Science Camp who had become each other's family. Cheerful, Hebrew, conversation flew across the room interrupted, only so that the religious amongst them could bless the Sabbath.

And the second? Well, that was the night Jack invited the class to his home.

Chapter 7: December

In London I pause and reflect as this book begins to approach its end. When I look back at the rather pensive opening, I am delighted that the words startle me. My world has grown brighter with each passing month and rarely do I feel as despondent. At times I've even glimpsed my former self, been happier, more motivated, than I have in years. The world, on the other hand – well, that's a different story. A reprise of violence in Israel, fires blazing in America, Britain at odds with itself. I've tried writing with levity about my Thanksgiving in Jerusalem, but it seems jarring, what with Binyon's words still swirling in my head:

With proud thanksgiving, a mother for her children,
England mourns for her dead across the sea.

I must sing the words on Sunday, a work duty, in what has been a merry month of Kristallnacht commemorations and Armistice centenaries. My birthday fell in the no man's land between the two occasions, and perhaps it was the autumn skies (accustomed, as I am, to November being in spring) but I found myself feeling rather grey. Lonely. Sad. Wondering …

Wondering if there can be peace. Wondering if on Thanksgiving, this coming week, people will find things to be thankful for. Whether friends and family will lay aside their differences and break bread with a joy for each other's company. Or whether we have forgotten this in a world of such personal claim.

I'll never forget my first Thanksgiving. When I was six, my Dad undertook a visiting fellowship in Boston, Massachusetts and it was decided that we would join him over the Australian summer. I left school early that year for, rather than waiting for December, we flew out of Sydney in time to join my aunt and her family in New York for the November holiday.

What splendour! While my aunt roasted a turkey too large for her Manhattan kitchen, we strolled through Central Park delighting in the coloured leaves, the cheeky squirrels and how our breaths made mist in the air. For years afterwards, I smugly believed I'd experienced something few Aussies knew about. Returning to the apartment, we were thrown into a frenzy of activity, stories, a play, the sense that there was so much to do and not enough time. I tried to alleviate this feeling by asking what seemed a logical question:

'Can't we finish this tomorrow?'

Laughter.

How was I to know that it's only Jewish festivals which go for two days?

As fate would have it, the next time I had cause to mark Thanksgiving, the celebrations were spread over two nights. By a peculiarity of the calendars in 2013, when I was living with Americans in Israel, Thanksgiving and the first day of Chanukah happened to coincide (an allegedly once off phenomenon). With that Thursday being very much a work day, Thanksgiving celebrations were reserved for the evening with a festive meal put on for those accustomed to the proceedings, and those merely curious. An impasse, however, was reached when our philosophy lecturer, Jack, invited our class to celebrate Chanukah in his home in what was his own, unwavering, tradition.

Several of my classmates could not forego their turkey but my friends and I reached a compromise. Leanora and I would attend Jack's party while Sandy and Tanya attended the student dinner, postponing our communal celebrations to Saturday night.

'This way we'll have more time to cook,' they justified, masking disappointment.

As the day grew nearer, it dawned on me that, aside from the festivals, I had not been inside a home since arriving in Jerusalem. Excitement mingled with nerves as I tried to predict how the evening would play out. Would we have to make clever conversation? What were we meant to wear? To add to my anxiety, I innocently headed into the city to watch my friend in a dance performance, not calculating what Chanukah would add to the city's already precarious traffic situation. Having promised to travel to Jack's with Leanora, I jumped on the first bus that came past, praying that it was at least heading in the direction of the student village.

Home at last, I threw on clean clothes and headed with Leanora back towards the city, then onto a bus which should have stopped just outside Jack's home. In my haste, however, I'd written down his address but not looked at a map and as the bus turned onto Ha-Rav Herzog Street, I realised that we were on one of the longest streets in Jerusalem. With no knowledge of where, along its length, we were meant to be.

It was a taxi that, eventually, dropped us at our location by which time I was so stressed I'd almost forgotten to be nervous. Climbing up to Jack's apartment we found ourselves in a place that can only be described as cozy and all the more so for being greeted by Jack's smiling wife and four youngest children.

One by one, we lit *chanukiot* (two candles each for this second night) before taking seats in the lounge in a somewhat orderly circle. I found myself opposite Jack and, as latkes and donuts were passed round, found his gaze unsettling. I knew he'd read my paper. He was not smiling, nor threatening, so what did his look mean?

The question of the evening was what we had taken from our time in Israel. The strange thing is that as vivid as my pictorial memories are of that evening, from the red dress of my Chinese classmate to my English colleague with her child on her knee, I cannot remember what I said, let alone anyone else. I know the answers were insightful, we were a philosophy class after all, and I retain a nostalgia for the specific honesty and maturity possessed by the group, but it is as if the sound has been cut from the tape, returning only at the point when Jack began to speak.

We asked him a simple question: what class do you teach next term. We spoke, unexpectedly, of peace.

Like so many students, we had forgotten to consider that our teacher had a life outside the classroom. Jack not only hoped to open the minds of the future generation, but he actively pursued understanding the mindset of the current one. 'It is America,' he explained, 'which has propagated the notion that peace is Peace, and this blanket notion is Israel's greatest obstacle.' As the slogans graffitied on the pavement for John Kerry's visit informed us, it was also inflammatory.

However, more than simply realising that peace for Palestinians and Israelis might be a variable entity, Jack worked to forge communication across the Israeli political spectrum. That each party (there were 12 in The Knesset in 2013) might define the term differently was Jack's insight and, working behind the scenes, he sought to understand each agenda so as to counsel factions or, where possible, broker negotiations. Better to have winter sparks than summer fires, Jack explained, for the measure of his work was not what he achieved but what he prevented.

The Torah is a strange book for its brute honesty as regards man's struggle with man. Cain kills Abel, Abraham banishes Ishmael, and Jacob and Esau find themselves at war. These transgressions are easy to remember yet the prohibitions taken from the parables, less so: that men with unfulfilled contracts (be that to a house unsettled, land unharvested or a fiancée unmarried) may not fight, and that no war may be waged before there has been an attempt at peace.

We will remember them.

But not that.

Though we must try. For if our time in Israel had taught us anything, it was that we must at least strive to have an impact on the world.

***

Two days later we gathered in my apartment for Thanksgiving.

Tanya, Sandy and I had cooked all afternoon. Sweet-potato had been mashed, topped with marshmallows and placed under the grill. Green beans had been stringed and boiled, a chicken stuffed into our toaster oven and coaxed into roasting. Cinnamon perfumed the air, corn bread steamed on the table and wine was opened, even if it did not quite flow.

Four candles burnt in our foil *chanukiah* and five, very different, women sat in its glow. Four from America, one from Australia. One and a half Christians and three and a half Jews. Nothing, but circumstance, would have brought us together and yet there was no one, in that moment, with whom I would have rather been. For in spite of all our differences we were unanimous in our feeling, of gratitude. For the experience, for our friendships and for this simple, domestic moment of joy. And peace.

***

On Sunday mornings, as was our ritual, Tanya would meet me at my apartment (she lived four floors above) and together we'd walk to Aroma café. We'd chat about her boyfriend troubles, sipping iced coffees, discuss my sister's approaching visit, throwing our cups in the bin. Then we'd cross Churchill Boulevarde – did we need to shop that evening? Walk through Hadassah's gates, pause in our conversation for Security, close up our bags, walk through the main doors, a hug on parting, 'text me before you leave,' as Tanya headed to her office and I to the ER.

I'd left the student village as myself, with a young person's agenda and a young person's woes. But now, at the bank of chairs most empty at this early hour, I'd stop and open my bag once more. And from it, I'd take out my white coat. Put it on over my regular clothes. And suddenly you had cause to call my name:

Rohfah, rohfah!

(Doctor, doctor!)

Slichah, aval ani loh rohfah, ani rak mitnadevet E.K.G...

(Sorry, but I'm not a doctor, I'm just an ECG volunteer...)

Beseder, aval ani tzarich ezra.

(OK, but I need help.)

Given the demands of an emergency room, it was strange to have a job so singular, and in the stretches of nothingness, it took effort to quash the voice that said, 'Perhaps I could lend a hand'. Yet, it was this same singularity that ensured my job was never routine. A blood collector deals with veins and elbows whereas my domain was the chest and, in any context, but especially a religious one, this made each case an event.

Unbuttoning, unfastening, peeling back the layers …

The only time I saw male patients was in the hour before Larry arrived, and the few weeks when he was on leave, so the memories are fewer but prominent:

The middle aged, Orthodox Jew, who lifted up layers of unwashed clothes, untucking his white shirt from black pants, as I tried to slide the device under his *tzitzit*.[42]

The young attractive soldier, who asked if the procedure would hurt. His was perhaps the first man's skin I'd touched since maturity. I told him to take deep breaths to still his tachycardia and was glad the machine hadn't been placed on me.

In contrast, and unlike in my day-to-day life which was spent with women, at Hadassah my colleagues were men. And having grown up in a co-ed environment, I realised how much

---

[42]A fringed garment worn under the clothes by observant Jewish males.

I missed their company. And how this mattered more to me than their other defining feature, that they were Arab.

Faiz was a charmer. He flirted with the female nurse, scarf on her head, ring on her middle finger, she was married, Jewish, and, with no ambiguity, utterly free.

Farooq was bright. I always wondered if he'd wanted to be a doctor. Or still hoped to be. I learnt so much from watching him, his deftness, precision, and it was he I called in an emergency, when a nun three times my size needed to be kept upright to stay alive and I, propping up her body, trying to stop her eyes rolling back in her head, could not lift her, and her fellow sister rushed in, wondering what was happening, and I realised they only spoke French. I clutched my breast and shouted '*le coeur, le coeur*' and at this she ran across to help but she was even slighter than me and finally Farooq arrived, used the bedsheet to help move the body and told me off for being a fool.

I watched him fall in love. How over the course of a frantic morning, he got to know a woman, seated patiently in the waiting area, in a beautiful red hijab, who slipped him her number before leaving. Which he put in his scrubs pocket. And he must have called, for I saw them together a few weeks later and it brought me the greatest joy.

For that was what I learnt to do while waiting. To sit on my hands and watch. To learn the rhythms of the ward, the tubes sent in the vacuum chute, the midday clang of the soup trolley, the patter of feet, beds stripped and changed, a world aiming for stasis, before the doors would burst open and in would enter the unknown.

When it was very quiet, I read, a select list of things small enough to fit in my square coat-pocket. However, I rarely got much reading done for if it were *that* quiet, then Samer would join me. I'd sit in the patient's chair, he on the bed, creasing the paper I'd freshly laid, and we'd talk about what a girl like me was doing in a place like this. And he told me I was beautiful. And I never knew quite what to say. So I would just ask him about the house he was building. In the same village as his parents, and grandparents, whilst he teased me that my family lived all over the world. And I wondered which woman he'd take home to the house he built with the same hands which tended, so gently, the sick. Who would get to know this complex man?

For there were so many women. Muslim women, Sephardi women, Ashkenazi women, a woman from the clinic who'd come all the way from Tel Aviv. She didn't need to tell me; her red hair and black leather jacket would have been incongruous in Jerusalem. In a Russian accent, she made clear her distaste for being amongst the sick and I, trying not to laugh, just asked if she might prepare herself.

'I'm ready,' she said.

And she was. For she unzipped her black jacket to reveal nothing but a skimpy bra underneath.
Pale flesh, dodgy heart. I'll never forget the first time I, unknowingly, did an ECG on someone with a pacemaker. To see

the organic lines replaced by one of mechanical precision. To marvel that we, as humans, could be such clever engineers.

... of life, or our own demise. In would walk my women patients, tall and elegant, in coats buttoned up to their coloured hijabs which tobacco-scented fingers would now undo. Slowly they'd undress, for under public modesty lay personal comfort (soft pyjamas concealed beneath those coats) and under the personal lay the private world. Black lingerie, intricately fastened.

Their hearts were fine, I'd tell them in broken Hebrew which rarely matched their own. And then they'd cough. So I'd gesture against smoking. And this they understood, but chose not to accept.

The woman in the white coat. You can go wherever. To the surgical bays where three men stand around one woman and I, with the aid of a hospital gown, do my best to uncover as little of her nakedness as possible. To the infectious ward, where a woman with flaking skin and falling hair, sits upright and half undressed. I don mask and disposable clothes and wish I could at least understand what I'm being exposed to.

But the words float around, over me, between me, Arabic and Hebrew, the language barrier giving greater privacy than any hospital curtain. It keeps me working, it keeps me numb, eyes compensating for what the ears can't do. On alert and noticing ... noticing the two women sitting in bed, each alone, with no facility to penetrate the silence.

Oh God, explain yourself. Though I know that is not your duty …

In this world, it was English which melted my resolve. The American patient who insisted I wash my hands within her sight, and then complained that these same hands were cold. The visiting relatives who were so adamant that they could not be ill on holiday. But life doesn't always play fair as I learnt when a young New Zealander was brought in.

Under 40, fit and active, tended to by a loving wife. He was hungry, kept asking if he could eat and it was my duty to repeat the words: 'Not till the doctor has seen you.'

He was dying. He didn't know. He had to have surgery. Perhaps it saved him. I never heard.

To keep him calm, I let him talk. About his work as a guide of Anzac sites. He told me all about the Battle of Beersheba, about the miracle of the Australian charge, of how we should be proud of this great victory.

A victory for the Empire, against the Turks, which had put us where we were that very day.

Oh, how the British Mandate has become an inconvenient truth. Not just the Balfour Declaration, with its chaos of ambiguity, recognising that local Palestinians should keep their rights and foreign Jews not be persecuted for the Zionist cause – but the fact that Britain, a colonial power marched into Jerusalem in 1917.

And held the reins of peace and prosperity for 30 years – with changing minds and agendas because their decisions did not affect their people. And the cause was power and the people merely pawns, until something so unthinkable happened to the Jews that something else had to be done, and that something was Israel.

We see the coat, but not what it conceals. And few, save my Russian lady, come naked underneath.

***

Is snow in the desert a blessing or a warning? I still cannot decide. For while it beautifies, it also exposes cracks. Divisions. It can lower people to their most base or make heroes out of them.

On Wednesday afternoon, in the second week of December, I stood at the bus stop and realised that, for the first time, I was cold. Leaves and dust swirled in the wind as I hugged my scarf tighter, thanking Mum for her foresight: the gloves she'd sent had arrived that morning.

I shivered. Could the bus not hurry up!? I had to get home to write my essay – I should have finished it that night. But knowing that class was cancelled the next morning, I went to bed before it was done. I longed for the day when I'd make better use of extra time, instead of holing myself up in my room, eating chocolate and sitting cross-legged on my single bed, tip-tap-typing because I could not divorce myself from deadlines. Had I known, I might not have. But I did not know, none of us did, or none of us quite believed that it was about to snow in Jerusalem. And that we wouldn't be going anywhere for almost a week.

Even these five years later, I can remember being in the strangest mood. Irritable, singularly focused, not wanting to be disturbed. So it was snowing! But did people have to shriek about it, and right outside my window?

What caused my ire? Were my own insecurities creeping in? Fear that whatever I wrote for Jack would, after the Derrida paper, be insufficient. That he would expect further invention. Or would I, my ego discontent?

Was it self-protection? My friends and I had but two weeks left together. Were these walls to avoid future hurt. Or was it the question? That Jack had asked why, through Heschel's eyes, the Jews needed Israel. And I didn't bloody know.

Knock, knock. Tanya: 'Sorry, I know I'm disturbing you …'

'Yes?'

'Sandy and I are heading to the Old City. Wanna come?'

'No, I have to finish this.'

So the Kotel was dusted with snow! I'd seen the cars turned white this morning. Proof enough; who needed postcard views?

'You, Nicky,' would have been the answer, 'you who seeks beauty and adventure.'

But not that day. On that day I was rude, insufferable, for I would not speak the truth.

Just as I did not answer Jack's question.

Skirting round it, dealing with the parts I was comfortable with, avoiding with intellect what I would not confront with emotion (not that Jack was fooled). The more time I spent in Jerusalem, the more it confused me. The more it became my 'home', the less it became 'Israel'.

So, rather my garden be white than the forecourts of the temple. Rather the Jews live in Israel than need Israel,

Though that sentence is indefensible.

Instead of seeing Jerusalem, I wrote about it. Not from my perspective but the great Hildegard von Bingen's. Poet, mystic, philosopher.

I'd set her words to music.
A timelessness captured
In modern form.
Reused
To enter that same city,
Of which she wrote.
The city where Jesus died, and thus came to be,
Messiah.

To that end, I quoted Messiaen. Olivier, the great composer. Imprisoned in Stalag VII-A, he questioned life, and time,

And wrote a piece that sought to put into sound what cannot be put into words, using birds as a symbol for that which cannot be pinned down, but yet is universally recognisable.

Hope. Anguish. Pain.

To me his way of seeing was so like Heschel's. Two men fascinated by the messiah. But one believing he had already come, and the other still waiting.

For we can only wait. The Jewish connection with God being found not through his son, but through the Sabbath, *our* bride. For six days we toil, but on the seventh we enter the world of the divine, and in honour of this we sing.

Greeting the Sabbath, praising the Sabbath …

In bygone times, men would go into the fields of Tsfat to usher her in.

In Tel Aviv, today, the beach rings out with the sound of drums.

Music cannot sanctify. But it can beautify, coercing us to a higher plane, as close as we can get to holy.

For that was what Heschel believed,

That, 'The holiness of the Sabbath preceded the holiness of

Israel. The holiness of the land of Israel is derived from the holiness of the people of Israel.'

Kadosh,

Sanctus,

Muqadas,

Surb. [43]

I failed Jack. Unable, or afraid, to extract from those words a need for Israel. What I did know is that I needed music. And that all four quarters of Jerusalem turn white when it snows.

***

I had not long since finished my essay when my mobile rang.

Galit: 'Nicky, can you come to Hadassah? No one can get there, but you can walk. *Nachon*?' [44]

Nachon. Raincoat over my jacket, I headed out into the snow. And sat in Hadassah's Emergency Room, my wet socks beneath the chair, watching as more and more snow fell.

It was a quiet afternoon. Both staff and patients alike could

---

[43]Holy in Hebrew, Latin, Arabic and Armenian, corresponding to the four quarters of the Old City: Jewish, Christian, Muslim and Armenian.
[44]Meaning 'correct', *nachon* is used as both a question and answer as with the French ça *va*.

not reach the hospital. I chatted to Samer and then, unneeded, went home.

Walking carefully down un-swept paths. Back to the warmth of my apartment where a cat had taken refuge. Where, for as long as my allergies permitted, we allowed him to stay, until I could cope no longer and Sandy would get the dustpan, scoop him up (he was feral, after all), and deposit him back outside. Where he'd await the door's re-opening, and scurry back inside.

We named him Sahari.[45]

And it continued to snow.

All night as I sat on the phone to Australia, sorting out my timetable, not wanting to confront my return.

Through till the morning, when I rose and realised I hadn't shopped. And friends who'd meant to visit relatives kept calling to ask whether I could feed them, instead.

Of course.

With trepidation, I walked. Past pine trees suiting their purpose, white and green against the yellow of the Jerusalem stone glowing extra bright.

The guard shivered in his booth, scarf pulled up around his mouth as I, one foot in front of the other, wished for a guiding

---

[45]From *sahar*, crescent.

hand.

To arrive at the supermarket only to find it barren. Shelves raided, unreplenished. Women diving for the remaining supplies. I claimed mine: flour, chicken, wine. It was to be Shabbat, after all.

The right side of my jaw ached, my head was starting to feel light as I made my way back to the village, slipping, but not falling, heart pounding, finally making it home before collapsing onto the couch. The valiant fool with a migraine so bad I could not bear to move.

It was on that Friday that I learnt to ask for help. And that it was shameless. And that people will rise up when you permit them. Which was the most important lesson of all.

***

The city slept through that Shabbat, waking on Sunday morning to ask itself the question, what should we do now?

The universities were closed, the shops still empty, buses brought to a standstill. Arab men threw snowballs in the street, plastic bags tied round their fair-weather shoes.

I arrived at Hadassah to find the staff unchanged from when I'd left on Thursday. They sat on empty beds, slumped, utterly exhausted. And I'd been comfortably home. I felt such guilt.

They rested while I sat, waiting. I knew not what for.

The only noise came from the intercom, as plans were broadcast through, the disembodied voice far less comforting than the arrival of the physical Chief, beard swinging, bum-bag bouncing as he charged through the double doors with the promise of a bus to take them home.

They were saved from the onslaught. For the reopened roads brought with them every tragic case, at a rate so rapid the paramedics registered the patients, themselves, so that they could reclaim their stretcher and head back out to those still waiting.

Stroke victims, the mentally ill. Those defenceless in the face of nature. It was enough to make one cry. But there wasn't time for that indulgence.

Snow in the desert: a blessing or a warning, I ask you?

Chapter 8: *Tevet*

I'm writing these words somewhere over the Indian Ocean, flying to Perth after four months in London. And it feels strange that I can call neither home. In this limbo state, I contemplate how time can stretch, or shrink, so that days which languished become a moment, lumped together under the banner of 'experience', and I'm not ready to confront this when I touch down on land.

Things were never the same after the snowstorm. Not just because while our lives were paused, time had cruelly run on, so we found ourselves further ahead in it than we wanted to be, but also December brought with it visits from home. Tanya's family, my sister, Sandy's friend. And suddenly the world we'd built was shown up for what it was – temporary – as we slipped back into the space they'd kept open for us. For we hated to think they'd feel we no longer fitted, and yet we also feared the thought we had not changed.

It wasn't the first time our lives had been so disrupted. A month before, Sandy had abandoned us to fetch her parents from the airport and the three of them had driven down to Eilat. Before we'd even met them!

Two days later, I bumped into them on my way back from Hadassah. After the initial shock of realising how much Sandy looked like her father (John), and that her Mum (Mary) was even more upbeat than I could possibly have conceived, I noticed how much more relaxed Sandy seemed. She'd been nervous about their visit, the driving, and that they were staying in her room – but clearly two days of sunshine and familiarity had worked wonders and it seemed so natural that I invited the three of them to dinner.

There are of course many reasons why I recall that evening as being strained. From the simple fact that John and Mary were fatigued from their travels, to the psychological, as we weighed up reality against what we'd heard about each other, then to the more metaphysical, as two worlds that existed so well in parallel were suddenly forced into one. It is only now that I accept that it may just have been the strangeness of a 20-year-old hosting the *parents* of her friend. In doing so, I'd thrown the role they were so desperate to resume – carer, provider – into question, which meant we were mutually disruptive. But you can't see the mirror when your back is turned.

I merely muse. Though I do know that when Mary returned the invitation a few days later, Tanya and I found her far more at ease. She was also a woman on a mission, having promised us 'authentic' pumpkin pie and while I had wondered how she might achieve this, nothing prepared me for her retrieval of canned pumpkin from her suitcase!

The baking of these pies required the use of my toaster-oven, and so began the first of several journeys between buildings 6 and 7 (and up the 8 flights of stairs to Sandy's apartment) that took place that night. My oven was temporarily re-housed (or kidnapped, as my roommate termed it, for I returned to find him with a quizzical look on his face, bread in hand) and I was told to keep myself busy until Sandy called when dinner was served.

But her army commander rang first. I was sitting peacefully in my room when Jim barged in, 'Where's Sandy?'

'In her apartment, with her parents, why?'

'You have to get her. Our Commander's on the phone.'

With no further explanation, but a clear sense of urgency, I ran back down the path, up the stairs, and opening the door as I knocked, breathlessly exclaimed that Sandy had to come, and now.

Down the stairs, across the path, to my apartment where Jim's booming voice could be heard.

He caught sight of us, 'She's here sir,' and Sandy took the phone, discernibly nervous.

It was strange for me to hear her voice change, as she was addressed by last name, 'Arber?' 'Yes, sir?'

I tried to give her privacy, as she paced.

After a few minutes, and a final thank you, she passed the

phone back to Jim and told me, 'So I've got my assignment.'

Neither elation, nor disappointment. It was impossible to know how she felt. And what I didn't understand then, is that though she'd been given her role, Sandy hadn't been told to which base she'd be sent. And as it turned out, that came to matter more.

Sandy's parents were less ambivalent; they had decided where they felt she was destined, and like all parents were frustrated that others had not seen what they took to be self-evident. But we didn't dwell on it. It wasn't the time or place. Instead, Tanya was called, dinner was served, and we went back to 'getting to know one another'.

Amazingly, I recall it as a pleasant evening, friendly and warm. But the unexpected invasion of real-America into our little world left a strange taste in my mouth. Israel had brought out the best in us, as individuals, but the intensity of the country, from the climate, to the landscape, to the people, had left little space for our other allegiances. A situation in which can surely be found a moral on tolerance, but all I will say is that I wasn't ready for the awakening.

It sure was delicious, that pumpkin pie. Truly authentic. But in a way that none of us could have foreseen and for that reason, I'd struggle to eat it again.

***

Even though I knew Tanya's family could only visit because

of Christmas, it was hard to believe that the holiday was soon upon us. No carols streaming out of every shop, no tinsel decorating the streets, December 25th was going to roll round and we wouldn't even know.

I'd spent a previous Christmas in Israel, on the school leavers' trip my parents had sent me on in the summer of 2011/12. There were many things I found uncomfortable about the experience but most could be put down to teenage antics, and was it my fault if I felt above all that? One thing, however, undeniably came down to ethos and that was the trip's Jewish focus. Sure, we were there to explore our heritage but to deny a Muslim and Christian presence seemed ludicrous, and I felt this most when we pulled into a Christian town … on December 26. We'd missed what would have been quite a fascinating festivity.

In December 2013, it was my sister's turn for this experience abroad. Where I'd chosen a week in the desert, not being a hiker, she had wound up in *Gadna*, a military preparatory program, and so marked Christmas learning to shoot a gun. The thought alone was enough to make my stomach churn. My roommates, meanwhile, indulged in a truly unique opportunity. Committed Christians, Jim, Robert and his girlfriend Efa, travelled to Bethlehem to celebrate Jesus' birth at its very site.

To them it was one of the true highlights of their time in Israel, but it was a journey not without risk. To visit Bethlehem requires crossing into the West Bank and passing an Israeli checkpoint where each year security is tightened as Christian holidays have become all too common sites for terrorist attacks. Whilst Christian tourists are at least deemed to have cause to be there, for me to enter, a Jew, well, I was told that would just be looking for trouble. Without 'sufficient' reason, I'd be prodding a political situation that needs no excuse to stir.

Which depresses me.

Just as the Wall depresses me.

For keeping people out necessitates keeping people in; and the wall limits the general freedoms of Palestinians.

Which, understandably, has led to an exodus of Bethlehem's Christians.

Which results in much finger pointing.

'They are leaving because Israel persecutes Palestinians,' thrusts one hand.

To which is replied, 'No, they are leaving because of the Palestinians. After all, the number of Christians in Israel has remained stable.'

'So then it's the wall.'

'No it's the government.'

And was it not Jesus who said, 'Let he who is without sin cast the first stone.'

Of course I would like to ask, what would have happened if Palestine had accepted the Peel Commission in 1937 which saw Bethlehem protected by International powers. Or if they had accepted the partition plan of 1947 …

But like asking what would have happened if Romeo and Juliet had not died, my question is futile (though I fear we explore the former more readily than my own query), as futile as the finger pointing which can only further division.

Two nations tangled up in history,
In fair Palestine, where we lay our scene …

Indeed, this is why I give credit to Banksy who, in his usual secretive fashion opened the 'The Walled Off Hotel' in 2017.[46] Besides acknowledging that the Brits had occupied Israel before the Jews, itself a rare frankness, Banksy's hotel attempts to use art and humour to not merely comment on the political situation, but to redress the fact that though tourists may visit Bethlehem, they rarely stay overnight:

'Israel doesn't want them to. Going back to Jerusalem keeps the money with the Jews,' all too present, the old stereotype.

It's easy to say, to conject, to hate … whereas it takes effort to say nobody's wrong, which doesn't mean anyone's right.

And creativity to find a solution which challenges the status quo.

---

[46]2017 marked a century since the British conquest of Israel.

And empathy to accept difference, and believe that two truths can mutually hold.

Unless we do not want them to … unless we have become so conditioned to disagreeing that we are almost frightened by the idea of peace. For what then would we have to shout about?

Enough, though, with politics. It was Christmas, after all, and as is customary in Australia, time for a holiday by the sea.

***

Every country needs its Vegas. A place of lavish entertainment, where money rules and morals are told to stay out. To Israel, this is Caesarea, a dot on the map halfway between Haifa and Tel Aviv and yet a world apart from either. As much today as it was at its inception. Herod's city, the only part of Israel now privately owned, was, in the 3rd century, exempted by the sages from Jewish law. Secede to protect was their logic then, and after 1700 years, and several conquests, the city has to its unholy purpose been restored.

Unsurprisingly, a visit was not on the school-leavers' agenda and what with Tali arriving for the weekend, and as I wanted to show her more of Israel than just my apartment, her visit provided the perfect opportunity to go to Caesarea. Besides, we'd be breaking her promise not to take public transport, which made it seem all the more daring.

***

It was late on Thursday night before Tali arrived. Traffic meant she'd missed dinner, but my friends had sweetly kept wait, knowing how anxious I was about her arrival. This was the longest we'd ever gone without seeing each other.

When eventually my phone rang saying she was at the north gate, I hurried to collect her, grateful to see that one of the friendlier guards was at the desk. To say I had befriended them would be too much, but I did greet the guards each time I passed in the way my Grandma, who knew her butcher's name, would have wanted me to. It was not to be noticed, but it was noticed, as I learnt that night, when the guard let Tali in without registering, saving me the overnight visitor fee. I was touched.

If Tali was nervous to meet my friends, it didn't show. Rather, she regaled us with stories from her military experience at *Gadna*, entertaining with her new-found fondness for discipline. She chatted as we laid the couch cushions, her bed, on my floor and all the next morning as we walked from the student village to the tram, from the tram to the *shuk*.

I wanted so desperately to treat her, feeling like an adult, but not meaning for that to make her feel the child. Baguette with French cheese, hummus from a hole in the wall where you sat at tiny tables, pita served in wicker baskets, places I'd never been, things I'd not allowed myself. Treating her, or me?

For Leanora, I bought quinces which forever perfumed my bag. I'd told her how to me they were the fruit of knowledge. Needing Man's heat. Blushing. I wanted to show this to Leanora, just as I wanted to show Jerusalem to Tali; to show, to share, to reveal myself, to proclaim an identity.

Did it resonate?

Time ticking, trains to catch, fatigue fighting me, inexplicably exhausted. I fell asleep on the train, arriving in Caesare dazed. Embarrassed. In the empty parking lot we found a cab, which drove us through suburbs to our summer-styled accommodation. The 'Resort', now abandoned, chairs creaking in the wind.

We were utterly alone, idyllically so, the moment pregnant with the promise of sisterly conversation. But my eyelids drooped. 'Excuse me,' I found myself saying. 'I need to rest.' Weakened, weakening, Tali now having to watch over me. And when I woke it was evening, and Tali was hungry, and I was to act as the carer again.

But I had no food, let alone the Sabbath's bread and wine, and so we went in search of dinner, walking along the road, the beach to our left. The streets were empty, and there was nothing along our way. Eventually we saw a light and, following it, we found ourselves in a precarious place, with a worn-down sign and a four-wheel drive running its engine. But the words read 'bar and restaurant'. So we went in.

For food, as it turned out, we'd have to come back in the spring. So I, who had no appetite, had a glass of wine and Tali, needing sustenance, found ice-cream in the freezer. And we laughed and laughed, finding a unity that un-holy Friday in a way we'd not often been.

***

The following morning, standing in Herod's ruins, a Brazilian tour group started to sing. It was somehow so perfect, a moment of universality that rose above the pain.

Tali and I whiled away the day. After seeing the ruins from every angle, we proceeded to calculate how little you could spend in a restaurant to be justified a table, alternating this more reverent seating with sunning ourselves on the lawn.

When night fell, the trains started up again, and we, like the rest of Israel, made the journey back to our weekday home. With every seat filled, along with suitcases and bikes, Tali and I found a place on the floor, next to a German Shepherd who, fortunately, didn't mind.

Before 7 the next morning, I'd returned Tali to the group. It was a goodbye caught up in paying a taxi fare. 'Your change, Miss.' 'I love you.' 'Thanks.' 'Take care.'

From Tali I went to find Tanya. She'd already left the student village to stay with her family while they were in town, and was about to fly to Amsterdam. But that morning wasn't one for sentiment, rather practicality. That I was happy in my apartment, she put down to it being co-ed and, seeing as I was not going to be there, could she not have it for second semester?

In theory: yes.

In bureaucratic practice, which the housing board saw as their personal duty to uphold: no.

You see, a contract cannot begin until the previous one has ended, which leaves a liminal zone. And when that liminal zone occurs over Shabbat, as Israel found in 1948, or, as in Tanya's case, when one is to be on vacation, then the only way to navigate it is to admit defeat – or bend the rules.

Either way, there will forever be consequences and so it becomes a test of priorities, of allegiance – and I was prepared to risk punishment for the sake of Tanya's happiness. To claim I finished work at 3, rather than 2, and in that stolen hour have my keys copied, far enough away so as not to raise suspicion but close enough to return, pack up and relinquish my lease by 4.

To then assume Tanya's identity, and in doing so discover new things about myself, for example that I'd requested for the blinds to be fixed (had I now?) and so had the maintenance man ask if it was nice to now live on the ground floor. 'Yes it's lovely,' I claimed, and, 'No, there's nothing else that needs repair.'

Just my sadness, that in three days I would truly leave and this sojourn would be no more.

The quinces cooked, their skins turning from yellow to pink, their smell from floral to fruit. I poured the syrup into a cup and gave it to Leanora to drink. 'You sorcerer,' she said, her smile clouded behind deeper thoughts. 'It's good'.

She left again to pack her bags.

That night the five of us stood arm in arm, on the border between roommates and people we once knew. Camera ready, we smiled, for the joys we'd shared, I on the one side, then the men, Leanora holding on to their shoulders to gain greater height. Behind us were the music scores I'd tacked to the wall. I hadn't brought a music stand and after a few months, had bored of the pieces that papered my room. Might Mozart find a place in the dining room, and Bach in the lounge, I'd asked my friends who were, at most, indifferent. Leanora, however, delighted in it. 'It's like living in a music box,' she said, 'and so wonderful to partake in your joy.'

Don't leave me!

But she left. As did Jim. And Robert went away for a few days and suddenly only Luc and I remained.

Time was running out as fast on 2013. On the last day of the secular year, I came home from class a sickly shade of grey. Collapsing into bed, my phone woke me several hours later.

'Should we do something for New Year?' Sandy asked.

'Why don't you and Brooke come to me,' I replied, calculating I still had four hours until I was required to be upright. Leaving the apartment seemed one step too far.

I'd barely seen Sandy since her friend's arrival, part of me jealous of their history. And their future. But the better part said, 'Come, let's celebrate,' so we popped a champagne cork to say we had and our sober evening proved one of the cheeriest I've had.

Like those Brazilian tourists singing in Caesarea, we were ignorant to our incongruities. Two country kids, one city girl finding no trouble telling stories so we'd see midnight, and then forgetting to stop, until it was half-past-two. And laughing, I kicked them out, because I had a test in the morning. And for once in my life, the idea that I might do badly didn't perturb me at all.

1st of January. 2nd of January. 3rd, time to go.

I packed my bags, clothes in the suitcase, books in a box. Pots and pans into my new trolley bag. Red and black. No hands to help, I needed wheels to live alone.

As I took down the music from the wall, it stuck and tore; Israeli blue-tack clearly of military strength. In horror I saw the blue marks left glaring on the wall.

'Don't worry about it,' Sandy said as the taxi called. It wasn't yet goodbye. I was rushing out so I could come back before Shabbat. The final supper.

Deep breaths. Into the cab, giving the driver my new address.

The Steps of the Visitation. Though no one would visit me there.

When I returned to my flat it was empty. I sighed, preparing to scrub away the last bit of any good feeling. But then I saw. The walls were spotless. Sandy's unspoken gift, more tender than any goodbye.

Chapter 9: January

Now the serpent said to the woman, 'Did God really say, "You must not eat from any tree in the garden"?' Said the woman to the serpent, 'We may eat fruit from the trees in the garden, but God did say, "You must not eat fruit from the tree that is in the middle of the garden, and you must not touch it, or you will die."'

***

Why did I move to Ein Karem? It is impossible to say for sure. That a colleague planted the idea that it was 'safer for a young woman to stay in a convent guesthouse than a hostel', and that one of these guesthouses happened to be in Ein Karem was true. But the fact that I had not researched any other accommodation was harder to justify. That Ein Karem happened to be a village, and that I had always wanted to live a village life was true as well but my colleague hadn't known of my proclivity when she made the suggestion.

For Justina, the Nun to whom I paid rent, that I worked at Hadassah was logic enough. That I was based in Mount Scopus, an hour away, and not at the hospital down the road was either overlooked or not appreciated. Just like the presumption that I was German and that, even if I was non-practising, I was descended from the Christian faith.

'Are you Catholic?' Justina asked, after I laughed at her joke about Jesus. 'No.' 'Protestant?' 'No.' 'Ah well,' she'd surmised, 'perhaps you'll find Jesus one day, but not now. I know, you're busy.'

It was a world of utter incongruity, that in a valley so beautiful could exist a microcosm verging on threatening, if one allowed oneself to be so suggestive, or at the very least, absurd. A world of unanswered questions, encouraging flights of fancy, sleuthing without the denouement. It's what makes it so difficult to write about, for without an ending how does one know where to begin?

Perhaps with the building itself, which was humorously sterile, less austere than sanitary as if the nuns believed that such a setting would inhibit sin. The décor was based on shades of green, beige and brown, the tables covered in plastic – temptation daring not to show its head.

Incongruous, therefore, was the large and jolly Christmas tree that stood in the main foyer (the day of Epiphany having not yet come). Around it, stood a ring of toy sheep, well, almost a ring, for invariably one was missing, claimed by the younger of Justina's two dogs as his own. This did distress Justina so, and watching her turn into Bo Peep, habit and all, allowed me to forgive some of her more questionable characteristics.

Chico and Groucho, as the dogs were known (did she know those comedians had been Jewish?) were both charming and a nuisance. It was because of them that I was curfewed, for they sure did try to alert the whole valley to my presence, but there was something quite comforting about having these little lives running around.

Indeed, it was only in moving to the convent that I realised that our life in the student village had been thoroughly devoid not only of dogs, but of children. Standing at the bus stop the first morning, seeing the kids dressed for school, I realised how much I'd missed this normalcy, that the *Kfar*,[47] with us students in it and retirees outside, was like a symphony with only the 2nd and 4th movements. I know, now, that I need to live in the midst of life's full cycle.

For that was the thing – life in the valley was utterly divine. Can there by anything more charming than taking a shuttle-bus with Franciscan monks? Or walking down ancient paths to find men lying in the sun surrounded by goats. A stairway from the valley up to the road was called *Madregot Gan Eden*, the stairway to heaven, and never has a name been more apt. As tourists visited holy Christian sites, I took coffee on sunny verandas. I befriended the fruitologist, from whom, each Friday, I'd buy a Sabbath treat, and eavesdropped on the counter gossip at the local store which, of course, closed sharply at 7 pm.

This was a world of morning frost and midday sun, of mingling languages and happy people. In central Jerusalem, vi-

---

[47]Hebrew for village and what we called our residence.

olence was on the rise, John Kerry's visit an excuse for publicised hostility. Barely a day went by when I could get into town without the tram being stopped because of a 'suspicious item' (which was less unsettling than the announcement not being translated into Arabic) and yet in the valley was a sense of calm. It was my protection.

Did I love it the more for the convent's chill? The steep drive with its double gate, the row upon row of empty rooms, the empty dining hall streaming endless Vatican TV. The nuns hadn't always run a guesthouse but the only hint of the building's former purpose was a faded painting on the garden wall. Was it the orphans who had tended the orange grove? Had the flowers been there, in their time, and who had lived in my room, in its wing set apart from the main house?

Perhaps it had belonged to a caretaker. Or maybe it was where the bishop stayed when he visited, the separate entrance providing the feeling of being kept in. Or out. There were other rooms, too. One that stood large and empty, another smaller one which stayed perpetually locked and a room I never saw inside, though I knew its inhabitant very well. He was a madman, in the truest sense, dressed in a coat and bucket hat. I was told he was harmless, but he did once try to taunt me by eating the butter squares prepared for breakfast. Poor thing, he was so rakish the extra fat was probably good for him!

Was this to be my Manderley? I thought so that first weekend as feet pounded outside my room accompanied by laboured breathing. It took me a few weeks to be brave enough to open the door, and realise that it was just the cleaner's young children, busying themselves while she worked.

Lest, however, I began to feel too comfortable, Justina would appear. She seemed to know my every move, chastising me one morning for not having showered, 'And the hot water was on specially.' When guests came on weekends, and I slipped a skirt over my pyjamas to pretend I was dressed, she would tell them that I didn't speak Hebrew. Thus any questions they asked me (which I understood perfectly) would be relayed through her. Why thank you, Mrs Danvers.

It was, as I said, absurd, and yet realising that I, unlike the nuns, was free to leave, I delighted in the mystique. Not enough, however, to confess that it was my current address. One night I stopped in at a bar for a whiskey, and as the bartender made himself friendly, he asked me if I had somewhere to stay. Yes was, of course, the only answer but suddenly I found myself unable to pronounce the words, *'Im ha'Achiot'* 'With the Sisters.' So I proffered that I lived at the hostel, to which I'd seen a sign, surprising the bartender who remarked, *'Zeh loh sagoor?'* 'Isn't it closed?'

***

Where lies the boundary between temptation and revelation? What makes us susceptible to some suggestions, but not others? It's the age-old question, if Adam and Eve had free will, what was God's original plan?

On the surface, Jack's essay question seemed easy enough: find a way to reconcile what at least two of the thinkers we'd studied had to say about politics and religion. I told him I might use music to bring Rav Kook's spiritual and Derrida's intellectual worlds into alignment and walked right into his trap.

'Lovely,' he said, 'but I know you can do that. Can you not address something more urgent, say something that matters?' Subtext, 'It's not enough to merely gratify yourself.'

I had the choice, of course, to say no, that it wasn't my responsibility, that I was just a student, permitted to be self-serving, and that I'd get round to helping the world when I 'grew up'. But I didn't have enough self-confidence to be a disappointment, so I wrote to Mum instead.

'What should I do?'

'Add a layer,' she replied. 'Keep the music – Derrida and Kook – but see what they can say about the women you've treated, these religious women at the face of a political struggle.'

Well, I thought, it sounded clever.

Inside I screamed, *But how?*

Contra punctum, point against point. Simultaneity, akin to how I'd learnt about it. A musical form taught by one teacher and read about for another. The latter's subject was post-colonialism. My discovery: Edward Said. Forgive me, I know it's clichéd, but I was fifteen, and teenage duty is to think one's being unique.

I had always loved classical music and it was in the 10th grade that my English teacher told me that what I'd played had made him cry. Finding that Said used music to make sense of the world was thus enticing. Out of all the theoretical frameworks, I had never found one that fitted, so the idea that Said's might have scope for me called me all the more. Was it my fault that I misread him, taking his analytic tool to be a framework it never was? Of course. But I was fifteen, so forgive me, once more.

Counterpoint became my antidote to feminism, finding a way to empower women without having to disempower men. Let men and women be interweaving lines, I suggested, simultaneously inter- and in-dependent. Let them play off one another, realising a harmony, but one that is heightened by the careful handling of dissonance. Tension that can be resolved.

To find Kook in this was easy. He insisted upon the complementarity of opposites, the broken fragments that made up the beautiful whole. Could I say, then, that in a similarly transcendental manner, Western society had tried to overpower extreme religious practice through condemnation and that, instead, change had to come from within?

But Derrida, where did he fit? All I could think of was his *differance*, situational difference, functional difference, rather than a change of identity. Could orthodox women be empowered by this principle? If a situation permitted them to be raised up, without having to forgo any of their devotion?

I thought of a piano, how the same note has different roles in every chord. Take an A, stack a C# and E on it and A's the tonic of the chord. Take that same A, and put an F, then a D, then a Bb under it, and it's the dissonant note, with a yearning that leads you back to the home key.

And my yearning, living now across the city, in a tiny room, riddled with damp, was it yet for home? No, my heart pounded, there's something yet, something more …

Searching, searching, reading, finding connections but nothing tied up. Fleeing my room in frustration, seeing my village abuzz, but not able to be in it. Circling around, getting nowhere, only depressed.

UN reports about gendered abuse. Punishments befalling non-virgins, while I visited sites named for the most famous virgin of them all.

Mary's Spring, where pilgrims gathered to wash their clothes.

Churches and chapels, and paths that I walked as I tried to make sense of the female plight. Why? Because it is said that we tempted man? But the Torah tells us that woman was taken from *hu*man's chest and only in forming her, did man become himself.

Having a coffee in a building of ancient stone, I decided to go back to the source. All musicians understand that we interpret a score. Might it be how we interpret the Torah and Quran that causes our trouble, not that which is actually written there?

And so the idea began to take form:

Let Religion and Politics be two interwoven strands, the interplay of which have defined our history and will continue to shape our future. Many in the Western world believe that they are so discordant the only solution is to separate them; but not equitably, in two domains, rather the 'rational' Politic should be dominant and the 'irrational' Religious should be submissive, saved for the private sphere. Others call for total unification; the Religious is the Politic is the Religious...

Now let us consider something more fundamental, that within these two domains are the interwoven strands of men and women. Here, society has urged us to recognise the inequities and imbalances between the two and, in the instances of Western democracy and Reform Judaism, have ensured that this equity has been restored. Indeed, in these cases, women can hold any position open to a man.

And so, in deeming this a success, society looks to Haredi Judaism and Sharia law and criticises the subjugation of women under these reforms. Indeed, there is something essential in ensuring that women have an equitable and meaningful role in these traditions. But separating the strands, where equity is a product of sameness – and perhaps foundationally, this desire is flawed – is not a model that can be applied in these cases because, in doing so, one would contradict their very history and framework. Instead, the roles of men and women should come to be understood contrapuntally. In reconciling these strands within a particular religious-political framework, perhaps then there will be hope of reconciling two such frameworks. After all, they too are interwoven lines.

***

I finished the paper. And spent the next two days in bed. It was as if my body had used up every last drop of energy and now it would dictate how my time was spent. 'Lie down, flat, lights off, lights on, I don't care.' Within the tiny room, nails on walls where crucifixes used to be, I tossed and turned. Everything about me was fitful, a train in the night, lights flashing past. Tossing, turning, panicked thoughts that demanded acting on …

What's making me so ill? Chronic fatigue? But then why am I so thirsty, waking, parched? If it's dust, what can I do? But it's scary to be so tired. So alone.

Inflammation became the only answer. Eighteen months later, the recurrent swelling I had in the fingers of my right hand became permanent. No direct factor was found but my aunt and great-aunt developed similar arthritic conditions and it could be concluded that I had some unfortunate genetic malady.

Rabbi Elazar ben Azariah wished for a grey beard so he could be perceived as the wise man he was. I, on the other hand, long for the frivolities of youth.

[Three years on, I'm invariably much better, but this is thanks, in part, to an increased vigilance. No symptom goes unnoticed. At times I verge on paranoia, because it doesn't take much for me to end up back in bed, and to me there's no crueller place to be. I thrive on exertion, and yet it is my undoing.]

***

Over those days, my thoughts kept returning to the paper I had written, specifically to its unifying feature, music. How natural it had been to write it in Sonata form, with an Exposition that sets out the two themes, a Development that takes these into twists and turns which, as wayward as they may become, suddenly achieve their logic in the Recapitulation, after which I remembered a composer could add a short Coda, like so:

To Rav Kook, it is the perception of 'God's majesty' that 'develops in the soul' that fills 'life with peace to the extent that the individual recognises the greatness of the whole and the majesty of its source'. Unable as we are to agree on the identity of God's majesty, Edward Said and Daniel Barenboim sought for music to fulfil that same purpose. As the great equaliser – of men and women, Jewish and Islamic – they established the West-Eastern Divan Orchestra to bring together musicians from Israel and Arab nations. Let us just focus on a minute aspect of this project, its name. A divan in Persian refers to 'a legislative body, council chamber, or court of justice'. Indeed, in many ways, the structure of the orchestra is an insight into politics best realised, where the two 'sovereigns', the composer and the conductor, must reconcile their egos to achieve the overall unity that requires the whole orchestra in order to be achieved. The audience cannot shape the melody nor enhance the harmony, they are merely witness to its achievement and critics to its failure. Thus, in looking towards the future we must remember that change – for men and women, religion and politics, Palestine and Israel – will only come from within. Let the audience vote with their feet but not think that they should be the one to wave the baton.

Jack had asked me to find an urgency, to write on something that mattered and I had become inseparable from the task. It was my urgency, my adamancy; it all seemed so logical, let music be our guide to co-habitation, our insight into interdependent existence. Let music say that two states are nothing if they don't form one state and one state is impossible without two and let us realise that we have to strengthen the lines, Israel and Palestine each in turn, before they will ever, possibly, hold together.

It was infectious, this belief, I was music's disciple, as I tangled myself in clammy sheets, learning what a night sweat was, coming to understand the stories of the saints. Miracle is a better word than madness, a vision better than delirium:

Conducting, Nicky, it was what you always wanted to do …

… but you know why I didn't. I don't like to work on Shabbat.

But you live next to a music centre now, and you saw everyone coming for the concert on Saturday …

… so you're saying if them, why not me? But I'm not good enough. I'm not a 'musician' just a hobbyist.

But have you tried? You remember when Nell told you she'd been to the Conservatoire. How jealous you were? Go on, look it up …

… conducting at the Conservatorium is only for post-graduates.

So make it a goal. Ha, you really think you could 'just go' next year …

… wait, the audition piece is Beethoven 4.

So …

… Beethoven. You mean I'd get to conduct Beethoven?

Conductors conduct Nicky, that's the point …

… Beethoven. Why did I never think of that?

Soft tears began to fall.

I dropped the thought into a conversation with Mum. Very much in passing. As a way, more than anything, of bemoaning Jack's hints that I consider a profession other than medicine.

'If he (you) is so sure it's wrong for me, why can't he (you) tell me what I should do?'

I echoed what I had so often thrown at her, attribution obscuring my admission: 'Because the only other thing I've wanted to do is conduct.'

We were caught in an ironic tangle, Mum and me. She was concerned a career in medicine was unwise, witness, as she was, to a father, sister and husband who'd pursued it. She wasn't thinking that I did not have the qualities to be a doctor but, rather, she was afraid that I would find it suffocating.

I, on the other hand, had not found another world that combined logic with the human form, that allowed one to work with one's hands and mind – for my singular goal was to be a surgeon. The happiest place I'd yet been was working at Hadassah, and if that was doing a diagnostic task, how much more so when I could be involved in the cure.

When I was well enough recovered, I caught the bus to Haifa to visit a friend from the science camp. Our two days were idyllic. For whatever spark it is that bonds people in a group, alone we discovered so many things in common. A love of the beach, even in winter, as we walked along the endless sand, and for hazelnut biscuits and cheese served with jam. That Deena had grown up in Germany I hadn't known, so that added to our Semitic relation to food and family, we shared a continental affinity. That was unexpected, and yet so delightful. To sit across from someone with whom you do not have to explain your prismatic identity.

That night we headed to the Technion dorms where we found her friend playing the piano. A man appeared, jocular and jovial, and we headed to his car and drove, with Arabic music blaring, for sushi in town. The three of them were medical students, I the aspirant, so we talked. I hung onto the man's every word as he, the eldest, had seen so much and spoke with such passion that I was sure my dream was affirmed.

It was one of the most normal nights I'd had in Israel, delightful in being mundane. And yet it would have been so different if I had been an Israeli and not a guest, an Australian. If I had been lumped under the banner of 'Jew', one who didn't always make it so easy for the Christian Arabs, that group in the gap, would I have been so welcome?

Justina had warned me to lock up, lest the Jews steal, 'and the Muslims are even worse.' The Muslim man who'd driven me to the convent had bemoaned the Jews and, having confirmed I wasn't Christian, hoped I might one day see Allah's light.

Was it the medicine I loved at Hadassah, or the fact that it achieved a harmony in all this dissonance?

Chapter 10: *Shevat*

Life is a series of collisions, where two people, travelling along their separate lines, suddenly find themselves in the same place at the same time. There are those who believe this is destiny, that they were meant to meet that 'tall, dark stranger' whereas to others, the universe is simply ordered randomness, and we merely players in it.

Fate, or happenstance? Whichever way you look at it there's something remarkable about these points of contact, because you can never know how your life would have turned out if you hadn't caught that bus on that day. And it's not only the major collisions, the ones we term anniversaries, that can have this effect. It can be the smaller ones, too, the ones we least expect, and even those that result from the most unpleasant of circumstances.

It was my second Saturday in the convent, the day of sanctity, or sheer isolation, when buses stop and no one answers the phone. My day began with a blackout. If not for it being in the whole street, Justina would have blamed my heater, which I so desperately needed to keep warm. Then the problems became more personal, my toilet was blocked. Wanting to prove myself a capable young woman, I dressed and snuck out to the laundry which doubled as a tool shed, where I found a plunger. Sneaking back, so Justina wouldn't see me, I got to work, only to discover a horrible truth about my bathroom plumbing: the toilet and the shower were linked, thus the more I plunged, the more the water level rose on the floor. I was literally standing in my own filth.

Utterly mortified, and not even prepared to contemplate a witness to my situation, I nominated a pair of shoes and a towel for sacrifice and set about cleaning up the mess. Only when the floor was dry, my shoes pushed into a corner, did I pluck up the courage to call on Justina.

'What do you mean the toilet is blocked?' she chastised. 'You didn't put paper down it, did you?'

'Um …' I hesitated, confused. 'Well, yes, toilet paper.'

'But I told you not to, didn't I?' Justina replied.

I only wished she had.

Thoroughly and unsympathetically dismissed, I went back to my room to await the arrival of the man Justina told me would 'sort it'. As the hours ticked on, I retreated more and more into myself, so that I was quite feeble by the time I greeted the man, who turned out to be the custodian of the music centre, when he arrived at 2 pm. My (short) dark stranger was probably in his late 40s, early 50s, and he spoke a good, if heavily accented, English. Against my warning, he tried the plunger once more and now there was no chance me hiding from my shame. But in spite of it all, Mr Custodian merely chuckled:

'It is certainly blocked.'

Fortunately, he knew where the pipes originated, in a shadowy cavity beneath my bedside window but crouching down there, my rescuer soon discovered how dark it was. Had I a torch? No. How about some candles? Well yes, though I did not tell him what they were for.

I struck a match, it went out. I struck another and it was just as soon extinguished. I had known that my room was damp but had not realised it was enough to stop wood burning. I felt the panic rising, the room conquering me until at last, flame and wick met. Arm through the window, I lit up the space as the custodian worked. He sang in Arabic. I changed arms. He tinkered some more. Then he pronounced the job done, righted himself and returned to my room. I held onto the candle, just in case. The toilet flushed, but I was more overwhelmed than relieved and, noticing this, the custodian asked me why I was sad.

'This was not a very nice thing to happen,' I said, more childish than eloquent.

'Perhaps,' the custodian replied. 'But you cannot be sad here.'

As we cleaned up, he told me about the music centre and, delighted to find me sympathetic, insisted I come to a concert as his guest. I thanked him, profoundly, for he had been more than a comfort. So I tried, the next week, to attend, as he'd suggested. But the concert was already full.

And so the days went on. The term came to an end at ELSC and I took my first exams shortly afterwards. When I came home after the second exam, and with 17 days until the next, I decided to take the afternoon off and explore. Changing into sensible clothes, all black, with a beret and scarf for the cold and sunglasses for the Israeli sun, I went out to hike the hills that led first to a monastery and then, up further, to the road.

At the bottom of my road, at the junction that is Mary's Spring, I heard a voice call out 'Hello!'. It was the custodian, and he seemed delighted to see me.

'Today you do not look sad, so things are better?' he asked.

'Why yes, thank you, that was just a bad day and really I'm sorry I've not seen you. I wanted to thank you for your kindness.'

'You see I told you, you could not be sad here,' he continued. 'Indeed, today you look beautiful.'

I blushed, touched, all the more for knowing that dressed like that, few in Australia would agree. 'Thank you'.

'Yes, you are an angel come to visit us. I think you will bring us good things.'

It was so earnest, so purely said that it has remained one of the most touching moments of my life. A chance meeting at the crossroads and yet for a moment I was permitted to believe in myself.

Soon, I was lost in nature, never quite finding my sought-after path, only gates locked against those without the key. But I still found a way to climb the hillside, along a red-ochre track, with trees all around, and birds, and a sense not of being alone but of being utterly free. Though the sounds of the road grew louder as I climbed, it was still with some surprise that I found myself soon confronting bitumen. A bus stop and a garbage bin. The hope had been to walk to Hadassah Ein Karem; where I was now, I hadn't a clue. But then a bus pulled up with the hospital as its destination and suddenly my meandering seemed far from that, at all.

Sweaty and dust covered, I boarded. A few sweeping turns later and we had arrived. The Hadassah I worked at was a people's hospital, whereas this was far more grand. But I decided to embrace my conspicuousness, feeling that day so proud. I didn't belong there, but I knew where I belonged in Jerusalem society. I had found my place so, when I left, it would be by choice, not compulsion, with a knowing why, but without closing any doors.

Here, I'd come to open one. Specifically, that of the synagogue which housed twelve of Chagall's stained-glass windows. When I was a child there were glass roses in my front door. I loved how the light played with the colours, how they'd refract, against the white wall, the cream of the carpet. Growing up, I'd visited many hospitals, my surgeon father with his daughter in tow. I'd misunderstood the reason for the chapels, wondering who would choose to get married there. I was from a country where nurses were called sisters, many hospitals were named after saints. An alternative to this Christian narrative had never been presented to me, and then suddenly, as a young adult, there I was in a country where hospitals had synagogues, where my shopkeeper, policeman and bus driver were Jews. And that was in some ways miraculous, to know what it felt, for the first time, not to be the 'other'. But it wasn't Israel as the Jewish homeland that, to me, made it striking. It was that the custodian of the music centre thought of angels. That there was a palpable sense of spirituality, wherever you went, and that people believed.

Three faiths lay claim to Jerusalem. From that city has sprung so much of the essence of our Western world. It was, and will forever be, remarkable. If only we would just stop fighting, and let it be the stained-glass window. Better for being made up of different fragments. And through which the light shines in an unimaginable way.

***

And then it was time to say goodbye. To visit friends in far flung places, but nowhere near as far as they soon would be. For a day I was a celebrity, when I chose to get my hair cut in Dimona (I blame the macaw outside the shop) and found that no one could quite believe an Australian was visiting their sleepy town.

I went to Tel Aviv to hear the leader of the opposition speak.

Arriving early, I walked to Jaffa, finding the port city all the more beautiful at night, and stopped and had a diet coke in an empty café. From the neighbouring shop, I bought a pair of red boots and chatted amicably with the salesman, who liked Australia, indeed, especially Nimbin.[48]

With boots in hand, I walked to the venue, discovering it to be a trendy furniture store. It was an event for new immigrants, so I fabricated a story and enjoyed mingling with other foreigners as we were handed cups of wine. We perched on chairs we could never afford, and a man teased me that perhaps that was the point, that in our proximity we'd spill the wine, stain the furniture and be forced to purchase it. I laughed, he laughed. He could flirt all he wanted because when he called later, I would not be there.

To return. I raised the question earlier of whether you ever can. Return home. Could I slip back into family life, relinquish this freedom, independence, where I could be whoever I wanted, a different person each night … feel I was truly Australian, proudly so. All this would cease when I got home.

Yet life in Israel would equally disappear. Friends closing over the gap you left, life going on. I'd stopped working at Hadassah the last Sunday in January, being glad Samer was there so I could at least say goodbye. By now there'd be someone working in my place, a new name to be learnt, until it wasn't new, just a name. And on and on.

I marked my last week in Ein Karem by eating ice-cream for

---

[48]A town in NSW known for its liberal attitude to marijuana.

breakfast, then hiked through the forest at the base of Mount Herzl to catch the tram. And I was reminded of the children's song 'Upsy Down Town' yet for me the sky was the sea, for everything, utterly everything, felt possible.

In that week I was disembodied. My family were in Spain and perhaps that's why I felt pleasantly untethered, with my head leading a life of its own. It was a sober drunkenness, where I could be numbed yet simultaneously see things with a greater clarity. Where dichotomies were apparent, yet they did not hurt in their usual way. Though they would, with time, for when I left this bubble, and reunited with my family, I would have to turn these thoughts into words, words into actions. I would have to decide ... between medicine and music. Each inextricably a part of me, the one logical, the other romantic, but neither wrong.

I caught the tram to the Central Station, and from there took the bus to Givat Ram. Four months before, I'd been so hopelessly lost; now I directed those on orientation before the second term. This would be one of the hardest places to leave. This campus, which eighteen months before had so inspired me that I pledged I would return. For its lawns to take lunch on, beneath the shade of a leafy tree. For its European cafes, frequented by a constant stream of visiting professors. And for its maths library, its rocky path, its bus stops. This microcosm of intelligentsia but with something distinctly Israeli about it that kept it raw.

For one of the last times, I climbed the stairs of the Life Sciences building to the lofty top floor. The lights were off, the rooms silent, the perfect place for Nell and me to study.

And so we did, my twin friend and I ... she who would remain at ELSC, having chosen this as her path, while I would head onwards, as yet uncommitted. We poured over calculus until we grew weary and then we opened the door of the small classroom, and turned on the light.

Against the whiteboard we placed a music score, W. F. Bach's resplendent flute duets. And so we permeated the silence, weaving a blessed counterpoint, for Wilhelm Friedemann, the eldest of Bach's sons, had made most use of his father's teachings. And pushed beyond it, exceeding it perhaps, so that his musical lines were more dissonant, more relentless and thus the players more in need of giving themselves over to listening, to sharing. To knowing that they had to enter that space where words were useless, that space of hope, and faith, of meals shared, and hands extended. Of grateful kisses.

> To a world without walls, or towers,
> no borders of hate and fear.
> Where harmony arises through difference
> the universal language rings loud and clear.

FROM THE SAME PUBLISHER

A Taste for Diamonds

A diamond theft. A fateful dancer. Passion, love and money in a story that unfolds through the rhythm of the tango.

'A Taste for Diamonds' is a love story that spans two continents, from London to Buenos Aires, as Harriett and the man she loves – the man who loves her in return – face the consequences of getting involved in the international diamond trade.

Not everyone's a good guy, as they find out to their peril.

Author **Diane Harding** plumbs the depths of romance and intrigue to bring readers a satisfying ending to a dangerous tale of love.

Category: BOOKS – MYSTERY – THRILLER – CRIME

An extraordinary relationship

Early in **Leo Ryan**'s career as a counsellor he became aware of the number of female clients being abused by their husbands/partners/boyfriends and was determined to help.

This book highlights his conclusions, making it possible for most people to bring on the changes needed have a great relationship.

Category: NON-FICTION – HOW-TO BOOK
            RELATIONSHIPS

Burma My Mother
And Why I Had To Leave

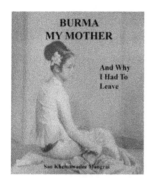

Myanmar's future is informed by its past - and BURMA MY MOTHER tells it like it is. A valuable story of living through good times and plenty of bad in Burma, now known as Myanmar, before an escape to a new life of freedom.

Author **Sao Khemawadee Mangrai**'s husband, Hom, was imprisoned for 5 years, and his father was shot and killed sitting alongside independence leader, General Aung San, when he was assassinated.

Khemawadee grew up in a Shan state in the north-east of Myanmar, previously known as Burma, and now lives in Sydney. Her sad memories are also infused by the beauty of the country and the grace of Myanmar's Buddhist culture.

Category: MEMOIR

Drenched
by the Sun

**I, who prophesy
by reading the stars and the wind,
now think of that country …**

Syam Sudhakar 'has an eye for the
strange and the uncanny and a way
of building translucent metaphors,'
according to leading South Indian
poet, K. Satchidanandan.

An award-winning poet who writes
in English and Malayalam, Sudhakar
is based in Kerala, teaching and researching Indian poetry.

Category: POEMS

BLACK, GAY
& UNDERAGE

In this first volume of a three part memoir, **Wil Roach** writes about living within a Caribbean culture in the heart of London, as a child of the '60s through to the '80s.

Born on the island of Trinidad and brought to the UK as a baby, Wil grew up as a gay black boy in the frosty capital of Britain, learning by degrees about cultural and sexual diversity.

Category: MEMOIR

I WILL

Unable to speak after suffering a stroke, **Jenny Sheldon** never lost her understanding of words.

Determined to regain her life, she used singing, swimming and her love of life to find her way back. This book is her triumph – and a compelling example to others.

Category: MEMOIR

Jiddu Krishnamurti World Philosopher
Revised Edition

The life of the 20th-century philosopher Jiddu Krishnamurti was truly astonishing. As this new updated edition shows, people from all over the world would gather to hear him speak the wisdom of the ages.

Biographer **Christine (CV) Williams** carried out research over a period of four years to write this ebook account of Krishnamurti's life. She studied his major archive of personal correspondence and talks, and interviewed people who knew him intimately.

Krishna was born into poverty in a South Indian village, before being adopted by a wealthy English public figure, Annie Besant. As an adult he settled in California, travelling to India and England every year to give public lectures that inspired spiritual seekers beyond any single religion.

Category: BIOGRAPHY

Night Road to Life

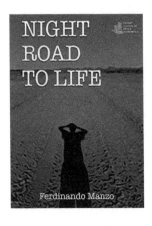

Themes of the sea and the emotions, particularly the deeply felt joys and melancholies experienced by men, are a touchstone of NIGHT ROAD TO LIFE.

Ferdinando Manzo's thoughts are not bound to fluidity; they fly to the greatest heights of exhilaration in poems such as, *The sky above us*, which displays 'a mantle of stars that burns in my heart' and in the evocative lines of *Eclipse*: 'the moon rose, bright between the eyelids of the night'.

Even the constellation Andromeda is given due recognition, breaking her chains and ready for revenge, before another poem *The voice of the universe* explores 'a hidden legend as far away as waves in outer space'.

A distinctive quality of this collection of poems is its musicality – the sounds of words carefully chosen, and their rhythms. The pleasing effect of the sensuality of sounds, ranging from gentleness to the drama of sex, is in tune with the gamut of human emotion.

Category: POEMS

Reported Missing

Di Harding's novel is set in a very contemporary Sydney, taking in multi-layered sights and sounds, from the northern beaches to performances at the Sydney Opera House. The plot spans the complications of what a woman must consider if she is to save her children from domestic violence. And the main character has good reason to hold fears for her life.

What would you do if your daughter was missing and you thought your son-in-law was somehow involved? Is there someone who could help you, or would you take matters into your own hands?

She does, and so the terror begins – from vile and personal harassment to life threatening acts, until she is ready to commit murder.

Her obsession with killing grows in her mind until she begins to plan and plot. Can she actually do it? Then something shocking happens to make up her mind.

The story ends on an upbeat for a new life ahead for the family.

Category: DOMESTIC VIOLENCE
                CRIME FICTION – SYDNEY NOVEL
                AUSTRALIAN FICTION

Road
to Mandalay
Less Travelled

'The Road to Mandalay Less Travelled' by **Ingrid Raj** provides research on a selection of Anglo-Burmese writing published from the period of British rule in Burma up until 2007.

What Raj shares with us in this study is the knowledge she gained about the value of social resistance achieved through writing. Both fiction and non-fiction texts are included in arguing a case that these might be viewed as tools of often ambivalent resistance against oppressive regimes, both local and colonial.Her research deserves a wider readership than was initially provided, and to this aim Sydney School of Arts & Humanities presents the work as its first publication in this new category of Essays & Theses.

We hope that specialist researchers as well as members of the general reading public take this opportunity to learn more about the culture of the people of Myanmar through their unique approach to storytelling, based largely on their religious understanding, their rich store of folk legend and their chequered history.

Category: MEMOIR – LITERATURE – BURMA – HISTORY

Road to Rishi Konda

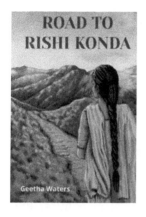

'ROAD TO RISHI KONDA' by **Geetha Waters** is a memoir of insight and charm, with a serious educational purpose. The author recalls delightful and stimulating stories from her childhood to throw light on the work of the philosopher J. Krishnamurti as a revolutionary 20th century educator.

At once fascinating and enchanting, Geetha Waters' stories centre on a girl growing up in Kerala and Andhra Pradesh in the '60s and '70s.

These youthful tales are underpinned by Geetha's deep understanding of childhood education, based both on her academic studies and in practice in her daily life as a mother and childcare professional.

Written from a child's perspective, the tales of awakening to life offer the reader an opportunity to appreciate how all children learn, as they draw on a deep well of curiosity that needs to be respected.

Category: BIOGRAPHY & AUTOBIOGRAPHY
PERSONAL MEMOIR – EDUCATORS

Stranger

Political journalist Nick Hunter suddenly loses his memory. He can't find his wallet, his computer password or even his name. When it comes to women it's even more confusing. Does he have a lover or a wife?

It doesn't get any easier when he realises his life is in danger as he's been researching a story on corruption at the highest level of political life. Things get even stickier once Nick has a 6-shooter out of his safety deposit box and in his hand, ready to fire in his own defence.

Set in the northern and eastern suburbs of Sydney where coffee and sex are almost too freely available, this story will sharpen your senses and set your crime thriller compass on true course.

Category: FICTION – CRIME

The Boots

All Mike has to do is get his mate's lucky boots to the stadium – but when Mike accidentally loses them his day is turned upside down.

Will he find them – and if so, will it be in time for the game?

In trying to meet the deadline, Mike has to cope with weekend crowds, hamburger cravings, a girl with a fox tattoo, Jedi Knights, and a bunch of footie supporters who are hell bent on getting their hands on those lucky boots.

Mike always thought Karma was a myth. But he may just become a believer.

Category: FICTION – ACTION & ADVENTURE –
SPORTS & RECREATION – RUGBY LEAGUE

The Dark Side of the Opera

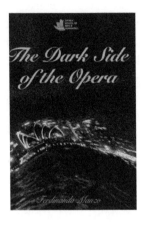

In this collection, **Ferdinando Manzo** plays with language, teasing out meaning and tempting the senses. His poetic approach is akin to the Buddhist path where happiness is gained through an understanding of negation.

From the earthly to the stellar, each poem holds the reader in suspense until the final moment.

Category: POEMS

Waking the Mind

Geetha Waters' engaging selection of short stories, 'Waking the Mind', is a reflection on Jiddu Krishnamurti's impact on her education based on her experiences at a school he founded in South India.

Geetha credits her passion for inquiry as being sparked the first time she heard Krishnamurti speak when she was six. That talk at the Rishi Valley School set her on an intriguing course of inquiry into the mysterious nature of the mind, the vitality of the natural world, and a creative understanding of life.

'Waking the Mind' is Geetha Waters' second book, following Road to Rishi Konda, her stories of a girl growing up in Kerala and Andhra Pradesh in the '60s and '70s.

Geetha Waters also incorporates the stories found in 'Road to Rishi Konda' in the STEP program for children and teachers in South India, a training module based on Krishnamurti's interactive style of relating with children.

Category: NON-FICTION – INDIAN STORIES –
PHILOSOPHY KRISHNAMURTI

What's in a Name?
20 People - 20 Stories

This collection of short stories will appeal to readers who are attracted to snapshots of the human condition. While set in Australia, the stories reflect universal themes. They range over a number of genres from crime to science fiction, from human weakness to human strength, and capture pockets of life with uncanny accuracy and sensitivity.

The author, **Lawrence Goodstone**, is a retired public servant who spent his professional life writing for others. With a background ranging from teaching to immigrant services as well as assisting in the delivery of the 2000 Olympic Games in Sydney, he is now in a position to write for himself and create stories from a life well lived.

Category: FICTION – SHORT STORY – SYDNEY STORIES
AUSTRALIAN FICTION

Printed in Australia
AUHW011904120719
314591AU00001B/1